CAMBRIDGE STUDIES IN PHILOSOPHY

Reason and value

D1219966

CAMBRIDGE STUDIES IN PHILOSOPHY

General editor SYDNEY SHOEMAKER

Advisory editors J. E. J. ALTHAM, SIMON BLACKBURN
DANIEL DENNETT, MARTIN HOLLIS, FRANK JACKSON,
JONATHAN LEAR, T. J. SMILEY, BARRY STROUD

Reason and value

E. J. Bond

Cambridge University Press

Cambridge

London   New York   New Rochelle

Melbourne   Sydney

Published by the Press Syndicate of the University of Cambridge
The Pitt Building, Trumpington Street, Cambridge CB2 1RP
32 East 57th Street, New York, NY 10022, USA
296 Beaconsfield Parade, Middle Park, Melbourne 3206, Australia

First published 1983

Printed in Great Britain by
Redwood Burn Limited
Trowbridge, Wiltshire

Library of Congress catalogue card number: 82–4564

British Library Cataloguing in Publication Data
Bond, E. J.
Reason and value. – (Cambridge studies in
philosophy)
1. Ethics
I. Title
170   BJ315

ISBN 0 521 24571 0 hard covers
ISBN 0 521 27079 0 paperback

RB

Contents

Preface

I remember being puzzled, as an undergraduate, when my professor and my fellow students all seemed to accept without question that only moral considerations stood in the way of doing what one pleased, and that otherwise there was nothing problematic about the pursuit of ends. One simply had desires for certain things, and if one could, and if there were no moral reasons against it, then one just went ahead and set out to do or get or keep them. Of course there was rational prudence, but that was just the avoidance of high-risk or careless foolishness in the pursuit of whatever it was one happened to want.

Here, then were a couple of dozen or so people equipped with a set of ready-made wants, which it was the business of their lives to set about satisfying, only taking care not to violate the principles of morality. I was certainly the odd-man-out, for I did not have any such set of wants (except the obvious appetites of course) and did not know what to do with my life. I wanted to find out what was of value, what goals were genuinely worth pursuing, before I could formulate a 'rational life plan', and that required something more than the consultation of my already existing desires or 'concerns' or speculation about my future ones. My fundamental practical questions were not 'When can I not do what I want?' or 'How can I best accomplish what I want the most with the least frustration of my desires along the way?' but 'What ends would be worth my while?' or 'What, of the things open to me, would be most profitable or rewarding?' and 'How can I realize the most worth or value in my life?' And this was something I would have to discover. The wants which everyone else presumably had, and which made these questions needless for them, I simply did not have at all! I thought I must be very strange.

I have since decided that I was not really so very strange, and that the question 'How should I live my life so as to realize the most worth?' is a genuine question for everyone, and it is not – almost the entire philosophical establishment to the contrary notwithstanding – simply a matter of working out an economy of desire-satisfactions.

In the course of my philosophical training, I soon forgot or repressed my initial misgivings, and duly taught, for several years, the orthodox doctrine, which for a time I fully believed, that wants (and perhaps ultimately only wants) provided reasons (grounds) for acting. The scales fell from my eyes, however, when I read Russell Grice's (as it seems to me) conclusive arguments to show that reasons (grounds) for acting are independent of desire (1967: 10–17). It was rumination upon this that led ultimately to the present study, and, I hope, to the resolution of that youthful puzzlement.

The introduction and the first six chapters were drafted at Cambridge in the spring and summer of 1979, the remaining two chapters at Kingston in the summer of the following year. The final revisions were made in the spring and summer of 1981.

Kingston, Ontario   *15 July 1981*

Acknowledgments

I would like to thank Professor Bernard Williams for the stimulus of his lectures at Cambridge during the Lent Term, and his seminar during the Easter Term, 1979, both of which covered material directly relevant to the present study; also for allowing me to have, in advance of publication, his paper 'Internal and External Reasons,' and for the benefit of private discussions. (Although we are in sharp disagreement on many questions, my indebtedness to him is very great.) I also benefited considerably from attending Professor G. E. M. Anscombe's seminar on reasons for acting during the Michaelmas Term, 1978. (I would not try to calculate my indebtedness, over the years, to her writings and her influence.) Thanks are owed as well to my fellow Cambridge sojourner, Professor Stephen Nathanson, for his generous and helpful criticism.

I am grateful to Queen's University at Kingston for granting me sabbatical leave in the academic year 1978-9, and to the Social Sciences and Humanities Research Council of Canada, without whose concurrent Leave Fellowship this project would not have been possible.

I would also like to thank the Faculty of Philosophy of the University of Cambridge for inviting me to give a course of lectures during the Easter Term, 1979, the preparation for which determined the shape of the introduction and first five chapters.

Special thanks are due to Mr. Jonathan Sinclair-Wilson of Cambridge University Press and an anonymous reader, for making suggestions that, I hope, have led to significant improvements in the text.

Finally I must thank Karen Hermer for her patience and efficiency in feeding my oft-revised typescript into the word processor, Christine Fisher for preparing the index, and my wife, Carolyn Dean Bond, for her valuable advice and her constant support and ⁊ncouragement.

Introduction: the problem

We do things, or refrain from doing them, for reasons, and we speak, in this connection, of the reasons *for which* a person did what he or she did. Here reasons are plainly tied to motives and – most would agree – thereby to desired ends (purposes, projects). But we also speak of reasons *for and against* (a different kind of 'reason for') doing things, reasons why we should or should not do a thing, reasons tied to the goods achievable by action (including evils reducible, eliminable, or avoidable), reasons tied to *value*. There is also the process of deliberation – the consideration of reasons for and against different courses of action, with a view to deciding which is the best or most desirable, and action in accordance with, or on the basis of, conclusions reached. This is practical rationality. Such acts, and indeed all acts done on the basis of considered reasons, whether or not they are preceded by deliberation, may be said to be *rationally motivated*. My aim is to investigate these matters: hence the title *Reason and value*.

There is a nest of possible misunderstandings that is perhaps best dealt with at once. The title is not to be taken as a simple conjunction; my topic is practical reason (reasons for action) and value (goods achievable by action) as they relate to one another, including all the complexities, entanglements, and obscurities that attach to this relationship. Untying these knots will involve some independent discussion both of reasons for action and of value (the good) and, I hope, will cast considerable light on questions both in motivation theory and in axiology.

Note: axiology. The present work is not, nor is it intended to be, a treatise in ethics, hence ethics or morality is not to be identified with the 'value' of the title. Since the central topic is the relation between reasons for action and value (the good) in general, where value is concerned it is the latter, i.e. value in the most general sense, that is at the centre of attention. Value, in this most general sense, is perhaps best glossed as 'that which is worth having (including

1

keeping and preserving), getting, or doing'. Of course the chief concern will be with goods that can be achieved by action (including the preservation of goods we already have), i.e. goods that can be obtained or preserved by *setting out* to do, get, or hold on to them. There are many valuable things, of which perhaps the most important is love, which are simply not within our power to acquire or preserve (except indirectly). That is why – should anyone wonder – so little is said about love in this book.

Ethics and morality enter from time to time because, after all, moral value is an important kind or aspect or dimension of value, and I wish to make certain claims about value in general, e.g. that it is always and of necessity objective, for which moral value would seem to present special difficulties. If, in my discussion of value in general, I am able to deal with the special problems connected with moral value in particular, this would have the advantage of clearing the ground for a *future* account of morality construed as objective and grounded in reason.

Some questions that must be confronted are: (1) Is every case of acting for reasons a case of rational motivation, in the sense defined? Consider, for example, that when we do something in spite of our belief that it is better or more rational either not to do it or to do something else (*akrasia*), we nevertheless do it for reasons in that we do it quite consciously in order to satisfy some present desire. (2) For a reason to be a reason for or against doing something, must it be tied to the agent's desires? Does every reason of this kind carry with it a motivational or desire component? A related question (3), Are we to identify value achievable by action with desire-satisfactions or some ordering of them? (4) Does every reason *for which* we act carry a value component? (5) What exactly is the relationship between value and desire?

There is a connection between reasons and value that seems plain at the start, for to believe that one has a reason for or against doing something, in the context of deliberation, is to believe that there is something of value or worth to be achieved (or preserved) by doing it or not doing it, as the case may be. And to act, or abstain from acting, on the basis of a reason one believes one has, is to act, or abstain from acting, in order to obtain (or preserve) the valued object. And, in such a case, the reason *for which* one acts, or abstains from acting (the first kind of 'reason for'), looked at from one's own point of view, is the same as the reason which one believes one has for or against (second kind of 'reason for') doing it. This is enough to establish a connection, at least in one context – that of successful deliberation – between reasons why one does (reasons tied to motivation) and reasons why one should (reasons tied to value).

It is the favoured view among professional philosophers at present, and I include Bernard Williams, J. L. Mackie, Richard Taylor, Gilbert Harman, and Rodger Beehler, that nothing can be a reason for a person unless it somehow relates to his or her present or actual set of desires, wants, or motivational propensities. This is because it is supposed to be a necessary condition of something's being a reason for an agent that he can be moved to action by it, that it be a *motivator*, and motivations require *wants* (Hume's principle), in the broadest sense of that term. (No want, no reason). But if to *believe* that one has a reason for doing something is to believe that there is something of value or worth to be achieved by doing it, then to *have* a reason, in this same sense, is for there to *be* something of value or worth to be achieved by doing it. And if reasons are necessarily tied to actual or present wants, then *value*, for an agent, must be tied to the satisfaction of his or her actual or present wants.

This is the pure doctrine. An agent can only deliberate on the basis of the wants she already has. Except for recognition of an object as possessing a desired character, and determination of the means to its attainment, reason and cognition are powerless to determine the will. Deliberation is of means alone. Bernard Williams is prepared to go a little further than this:

But there are much wider possibilities for deliberation such as: thinking how the satisfaction of elements in S [the agent's set of desires or motivational propensities] can be combined, e.g. by time-ordering: where there is some irresoluble conflict among the elements of S, considering which one attaches most weight to ... or, again, finding constitutive solutions, such as deciding what would make for an entertaining evening, granted that one wants entertainment.

As a result of such processes an agent can come to see that he has reason to do something which he did not see he had reason to do at all. The deliberative process can also subtract elements from S. Reflection may lead the agent to see that some belief is false, and hence to realize that he has in fact no reason to do something he thought he had reason to do. More subtly, he may think he has reason to promote some development because he has not exercised his imagination enough about what it would be like if it came about (1979: 20).

So, one may come to acquire new ends or lose some as a result of deliberation, but all such changes are nevertheless related to the more efficient satisfaction of desires one already has. Reasons are still wholly dependent upon the agent's present wants.

Thomas Nagel and Philippa Foot do not fit the standard pattern. Though Nagel would reduce value theory to motivation theory (1970: 5), seeing his task as that of showing how prudential and altruistic actions can be *motivated*, hence explained, he denies that we always act in order to satisfy already existing desires. *Considerations* of our own future happiness and the well-being of others (construed as the satisfaction of their wants) can motivate actions and, in so doing motivate the desires that are a logically necessary condition of their performance. Nagel's main argument can be seen as supporting the conclusion that reason or cognition *can* determine the will. He nevertheless denies, at least by implication, that one can make sense of *value* independently of motivation. One can take one's own future wants and the wants of others effectively into consideration in determining one's motivations, but these considerations are not justifications grounded in the recognition of the value of one's own future satisfactions or the satisfactions of others; they are merely possible motivators.

Philippa Foot (1972b) allows that the agent's long-range interests not tied to his present desires may provide reasons, but denies that anything beyond the agent's desires and interests, e.g. the good of others, can provide them.

Nevertheless the views of all those mentioned apparently have this in common. Ends – not only the ends that are actually sought, but those that are *worth* seeking (if the latter is not to be analysed in terms of the former) – have their source in wanting or desiring. Value, in so far as it is granted any existence at all, is the product of an agent's motivational propensities, that which determines his aims, goals or purposes. In the words of Rodger Beehler, 'Value is the shadow cast by human affection or desire (Beehler 1978: 143).'

I say these views *apparently* have this in common because there is one possibility I have omitted to mention. One can simply deny the connection between value, or goods achievable by action, what one should (or ought to) do, and reasons for action. Thus it might be true of someone that he or she should do something because there is something of value or worth to be gained by it, but false of that person that they had *reason* to do it, since they might lack the required motivational propensity. On such a view, value and what

4

one should do would be completely separated from motivation or its possibility. (No 'ought' would imply 'can'.) One could even deny that to believe one has a reason for doing something is to believe that there is something of worth to be gained by doing it. (One might claim that it was only to believe one had a possible motive for doing it.) But not only does the connection between having reasons and value to be gained exist in the language, it is difficult to see what point there could be in talk about worth or value achievable by action, and what one should or ought to do, if the connection with reasons, and hence with motivation, were severed. Properly understood, these value concepts would be useless in deliberation or any other practical context. Since talk of value or worth achievable by action, and of what one should do, is *conceptually* tied to action and choice, the view under discussion would amount, in effect, to a recommendation that all such talk be abandoned as irrational or senseless. Usually, however, (cf. Harman, Beehler, Foot) the connection between value achievable by action and what one should or ought to do, on the one hand, and reasons for action, on the other, is acknowledged. But it is denied that there can be any 'ought' or value or worth for an agent not tied to that agent's motivational propensities.

It is, in any case, a consequence of all such views (Nagel alone excepted) that there can be no reasons for action that are, of their nature, reasons for everybody or reasons *tout court*, since possessing the required (present or future) motivational propensity is a contingent matter; one may have it or lack it, as the case may be. And one consequence of *this* is that, since moral reasons, construed as universal and objective, apply to every rational agent, there can be no objective morality. And that is a very serious consequence indeed.

The views of John Rawls and his follower, David Richards, are significantly different from those so far discussed. Rawls (Rawls 1971) sees goodness as rationality, and rationality as action in accordance with a fully worked out plan that does not take times into consideration in working out a program of desire-satisfactions over a lifetime. The ideally rational man will order things so that he is able optimally to satisfy his desires over his whole life, preference being given to satisfaction of the greater wants over the lesser (frustration of the lesser over the greater), with no one time being preferred to any other. Any desire the satisfaction of which does not result in the lessening of overall desire-satisfaction (and the satisfaction of such a desire will normally result in the increase of overall desire-satisfaction) is a rational desire, one that it is rational, or good, to satisfy.

On this account, reasons are tied not to desires, *per se*, but to whatever desires fit into what might be called an *economy* of desire-satisfactions. It is nevertheless clear that, except in respect of strength, every desire is, of itself, on an equal footing with every other. If its satisfaction is *not* a contribution to the agent's good, that is only because it results in the frustration of more desire than it satisfies. Desire *per se* is plainly the source of all value.

Richards (1971) has principles of rational choice and principles of morality available to universal reason, principles which are to be understood as determining that reasons for action exist, yet which, even recognizing them, a person may lack any motivation to follow. In addition to recognizing that these reasons for acting exist, there must be a 'brute fact' desire to follow them if they are to be followed. Thus objective rationality and morality are saved, but at the cost of ridding them of their ability to motivate. On Richards' account, the connection between reasons and values has been severed. The principles of rationality and morality and the reasons for action which they provide are objectively and rationally determinable, but it is not necessary that anyone *value* these things, hence not necessary that they *be* values for anyone. Values, on Richards' account, are tied to wanting, and wanting is a contingent matter. Richards denies by implication the statement I offered as self-evident in my opening paragraph, namely to believe one has a reason for doing something is to believe that there is something of worth or value to be gained by doing it. But he does it not by severing value or worth from reasons construed as necessarily tied to motivation, but by severing reasons construed as justifications (as determining 'ought' judgments) from value, which, on his account, remains tied to motivation.

Thus we appear to have the following dilemma. If practical rationality and morality are a matter of reason or cognition, which are objective and universal, they must lack the power to motivate, since that power depends upon the presence of the relevant contingent desires. If, on the other hand, practical (including moral) reasoning is confined within the limits of the agent's contingent desires, there can be no universal or objective reasons for action.

Hence either objective reasons exist but lack the power to motivate, which seems absurd, or reasons are not objective but merely a function of an agent's actual desires. If the latter is true, then either worth (value) achievable by action, if there is such a thing, is the 'shadow of desire', or it has no necessary connection with reasons and motivation, which also seems absurd.

To put the point another way. Reasons for action seem to be tied, in some necessary way, to motivation, on the one hand (for how can one speak of reasons that cannot be acted on?), and to worthwhile things (valuable things) achievable by action, on the other, supposing that to see oneself as having a reason for action is to believe that something of value or worth is to be gained by doing it. But cognition of value, if it *is* cognition, would seem to lack the power to motivate, since that requires desire as well, and desire is a contingent matter. Yet there are powerful grounds for supposing that some things are worth pursuing and others not, independently of what the agent happens to desire, and that such facts create reasons for action. But if such 'reasons' cannot motivate unless we happen to desire these goods, how are we entitled to call them 'reasons'? Perhaps value is, after all, the shadow of desire.

Nagel (1970) would appear to have a way out of this dilemma. Not just the agent's *future* as well as his present desires create reasons for him, but the desires of *every* person create reasons for every person. Where there is a desire, present or future, mine or yours, there is a reason. And the understanding that such desires exist can motivate actions: thus it is possible to be prudent and to be moral. Nothing is said here about goods, only about reasons and desires. Nothing is said about value or justification, only about reasons and the possibility of action. Reasons remain firmly attached to desires. So whereas Nagel's account, if accepted, would show how universal prudential and moral reasoning is possible and can be effective, it is silent on the subject of goodness or worth, and that is because it is supposed that value theory, including ethics, is a branch of motivation theory, metaphysical though it may be. Ultimately there is no worth, only desire and its satisfaction. So this is not a true solution to our dilemma, which partly concerns the seemingly necessary connection between reasons and value achievable by action, between practical reason and the good.

It is the purpose of the present study to provide a solution to the dilemma, which retains, compatibly, both the necessary connection between reasons and motivation and that between reasons and what has value or worth, to lay the foundations of an account of value independent of desire, yet not severed from motivation, to clarify the concept of practical rationality, and to clear the way for an account of morality as objective and as providing, through universal values, universal reasons.

1

Desire and motivation

In this first chapter I shall be trying to get clear about two things relevant to the matter at hand: the role that desire plays in motivation, and what it is to do something for a reason. One of my aims in the first three chapters is to show that whereas desire or wanting and the reasons tied to it belong to the theory of motivation, where they are central, reason, in the sense of the reason(s) that a person has for or against doing a thing, is tied essentially to value, and the two are not to be confused. In order to present my case, I must begin with the matters taken up here. Their discussion inevitably leads to asking the question whether acts motivated by reasons can be said to be caused by them, and the related question whether and to what extent an agent can be said to be the autonomous originator of his or her own acts. Discussion of these questions involves considering briefly whether the account I offer of motivation implies any particular answer or kind of answer to two traditional problems: mind–body and free will.

To return to the central matters to be discussed here, there is a connection between reason, in the sense of reasons *for which* a person acts, and motivation, through a connection between *that* kind of reason and desire. Further, reason, in the sense that is tied to value, already appears at the level of motivation in connection with what I call *rational* motivation, but by no means in connection with every instance of doing a thing for a reason or reasons, a description which I claim applies to all standard acts. Exactly what I am saying and the reasons for my saying it should become clear in the course of the discussion.

I shall begin by claiming that every instance of a standard or paradigm human act is one done to satisfy some desire or want (I use the terms synonymously) of the agent. By a standard or paradigm human act I mean one that is conscious, voluntary, intended, and done for its own sake or to achieve some further end. This is the only kind of act of which it may be true that it is *done for reasons*, and that can be a matter of choice and decision, sometimes after deliberation.

The most obvious objection to this claim is that a plain contrast exists in the language between doing a thing because you *want* to do it, and doing it because you *have* to, whether you want to or not. Yet the things we do because we have to are just as voluntary, intentional, and purposeful as the things we do because we want to. Therefore (it seems) not all standard acts are done to satisfy the agent's wants; if the act is burdensome or distasteful, this cannot be the case. Of course if it is burdensome and distasteful but the necessary, or least burdensome and distasteful, means to a desired end, there seems little problem. We do it not because we want to do it for its own sake, but because we need to do either it or something equally burdensome or distasteful to achieve the desired end, and the flame *is* worth the candle. Though it is false that we do it because we want to, it is true that we do it to satisfy a desire, namely the desire for the end toward which we believe it is the necessary (or least burdensome and distasteful) means.

But there is another way of looking at this. It is surely a criterion of wanting to do something, in some sense of the word 'wanting', if we resist or sincerely protest if someone tries to prevent us from doing it, or if we attempt to overcome obstacles in the way of doing it. In such a case we can say that the desire for the end *explains* our wanting to do the burdensome or distasteful thing. So it is true that we do it not because we want to (which we do not) but because we have to, and also true that we want to do it in spite of its being burdensome and distasteful, this want being explained by our desire for the end towards which it is seen as the necessary (or least burdensome and distasteful) means. Since it is true, therefore, both that we want and that we do not want to do it, it follows that we are dealing with two different senses of the word 'want'.

It may look, at first sight, as if there is a broader sense of the word that includes desiring a thing either as a means or as an end, and a narrower sense that applies to desiring something for its own sake only. But this is not the true distinction. For one thing it would leave out the *moral* motive as construed by Kant (1785). On the Kantian view, we do not act on the moral motive if we act for the sake of something which we happen to desire, whether as a means *or* as an end. And, whether there is any truth in it or not, there are many who share this view: to do something on moral grounds is to do something, often burdensome, for some abstract good not related to the agents's contingent desires. At this stage we should at least leave this open as a possibility. But even Kant recognized that *some* motivational factor was necessary to account for being moved to act on moral grounds, beyond the mere recognition of the law, and he called that 'reverence' or 'respect' for the law.

The broader sense of the word 'want' is tied to this understanding that something beyond mere belief or cognition must be present in order to account for someone's doing something in every standard case of action – that there must be present some *motivational propensity* which is different in kind from belief or cognition. Thus we say, in this sense of 'want', that if someone did something voluntarily and intentionally, they *must* have wanted to do it, either for its own sake or as a means to some further desired end. There can be no action without wanting, in this sense. We say that a person wants to do something, in the other, narrower sense of 'want', only if he or she is *inclined* to do it with no effort of will, whether or not it is done primarily as a means or as an end. Nor should we forget the common supposition that something can be sought as an end, conceived as good, in the *absence* of any prior felt inclination towards it – an item affecting one's future well-being, to take the most obvious example. We may call the narrower sense of 'want', then, the *inclinational* sense, and the broader the *motivational* sense.

It is in the motivational sense of 'want' that I wish to claim that every act of every person is done to satisfy some want of his or hers. Still I do not want to claim that every act of every person must be done, whether as means or as end, to satisfy some *inclinational* want of the agent. Rather I want to claim that, in standard actions, there is always some desired end, the desire for which must enter into the explanation, though this desire need not be an inclination. However, where an act, A, is done only as a means to some end, E, for which one has an appetite or towards which one has an inclination, it is that appetite or inclination that is the real motivator. The desire (motivational) that we have for doing A has no existence independently of our inclinational desire for E. It is, as it were, a mere shadow or ghost of that desire.

Nagel would call the desire to do A a *motivated* desire, and the appetite for E an *unmotivated* desire (Nagel 1970: 29). Unmotivated desires 'simply come to us'; motivated desires come only after reflection. The desire to do *A*, like *A* itself, is *explained* by the unmotivated desire (appetite for or inclination toward) *E*. However, Nagel denies that every motivated desire must have an unmotivated desire (what I call an *inclination*) lying behind it as its explanation. Considerations (Nagel 1970: 30) of my own future well-being (desire-satisfactions) or the well-being of others can motivate me. Nagel grants that if I act, e.g. for my own future well-being, I must in what I call the 'motivational' sense of 'want', want to do whatever I do towards this end. He sees this following as a logical consequence of my (intentionally) doing it. But, as in the 'means–desired end' case, this want is a mere ghost, here a *logical* ghost, of the *consideration* that is really doing the work independently of any wants. The consideration (reason) that motivates (explains) the action also motivates (explains) the want. So while it is impossible, on Nagel's view, to do anything without wanting to do it, this is a trivial truth, for wanting to do *some* things, e.g. acting, out of abstract considerations, for the good of another, is *nothing but* a logically necessary condition of doing the thing, and hence (trivially) inferable from it. In such a case the work (the real motivation) is being done, not by any want, but by a reason founded on a consideration external to one's present desires.

However I am arguing that there is (that there must be) a real desire for (motivational propensity towards) an end at work in every standard case of action. In that respect I am in complete sympathy with Hume. It will not do simply to affirm that an abstract consideration can move me to act. For how is the connection made between cognition and the will? If reason and cognition are to be capable of determining the will, thus permitting an objective rationality and morality, valid and possibly effective for all rational persons, the connection must be made in such a way that a *genuine desire* comes into being *as a consequence* of the cognition or abstract consideration. Nagel's logical ghost is not such, and his account is unpersuasive. And surely we can and often do act for reasons, e.g. those tied to considerations of our own future well-being or the good of others, that are not connected with our present set of inclinations or appetites, the desires that we just have, what Nagel calls our unmotivated desires? At least this is a natural, common-sense supposition. If we believe we cannot, that is only a consequence of holding the view, outlined in the last chapter, that a reason must be a motivator, and a motivator must be a member of one's present set of wants. In this respect Nagel is surely right. And if so, there must be a way out of these difficulties.

In the case of all motivated desires, says Nagel, what motivates, or brings into being, the desire, is the same thing that motivates the action. Whether that thing is the desire for the end or the recognition of an external reason, *in* motivating the action it motivates (brings into being) the desire which is a necessary condition of the action. Thus the desire for the means *just is* the desire for the end; there is no additional desire. But there *is*, nevertheless, a motivational propensity to perform the act that is the means, a desire in the motivational sense of 'desire' or 'want'. While there is no motivational energy or force *in addition to* the desire for the end, nevertheless that energy is directed to the means. But in the case of acts motivated by external reasons (considerations), the desire, according to Nagel, is in itself *nothing at all*. It is a mere logical inference from the fact that the act was done. But if the desire is *nothing at all*, where does the motivational power come from?

Philippa Foot quotes the following passage from Nagel:

That I have the appropriate desire simply *follows* from the fact that these considerations motivate me; if the likelihood that an act will promote my future happiness motivates me to perform it now, then it is appropriate to ascribe to me a desire for my own future happiness (Nagel 1970: 29–30).

She then comments:

What we have here is a use of 'desire' which indicates a motivational direction and nothing more. One may compare it with the use of 'want' in 'I want to φ' where only intentionality is implied. Can *wanting* in this sense create the reason for acting? It seems that it cannot. For in the first place the desires of which we are now speaking are to be attributed to the agent only in case he is moved to action, *or would be so moved in the absence of counteracting reasons or causes* [concluding emphasis mine] (1972b: 149).

But the *point* that Nagel is making here is precisely that the desire is *nothing at all*, a mere inference from the fact that the act was done, a logical ghost *and nothing more*. And, being nothing at all, it cannot be a 'motivational direction'. Foot has got Nagel wrong. If it were a motivational direction, it would, as she implies, exist as a force even in the presence of counteracting reasons and causes that prevent it from actually motivating. But Nagel's want exists only as an inference from an action: no action, no want. It is a logical ghost that can play *no part at all* in the motivation of the action. That, indeed, is his point. It is not a *force* of any kind, since it exists in pure logical dependence upon the act's having been done. And if the act is *not* done, it has *no existence at all* and *a fortiori* no existence as a 'motivational direction'.

Yet it is certainly true, as Foot assumes, that if a factor can succeed in motivating an action, it can exist as a *motivational direction* even in the presence of countervailing reasons and causes. Nagel would have to say that the consideration, or the reason as cognized – that which motivates the act – *is* the 'motivational direction' that motivates the action or remains present as a motivational pull, even when the agent is not motivated accordingly. But a 'motivational direction' or a 'motivational pull', or what I have been calling a 'motivational propensity', just *is* a desire, in the broad sense – but a real one, not a logical ghost. If Nagel's motivated desire, in the case of an action motivated by external reasons, is a logical ghost, then this consideration or external reason (or reason as cognized) must *itself*) be a motivational propensity. But if it is truly a cognition, how can this be so?

We are forced to conclude that if we can be moved to act by considerations (reasons) not tied to our present set of desires, e.g. considerations of our own future well-being or of the good of others, abstractly conceived, these considerations must themselves *create* or generate the relevant desires. If the consideration (recognition or discovery of a reason) is a genuine cognition and not itself a desire or motivational propensity – and this is what Nagel wishes to claim – it cannot, as such, move us to action. And neither, of course, can a logical ghost. So, either the cognition *creates* the necessary desire or, as Bernard Williams claims, there can be no external reasons.

Appetites or inclinations – what Nagel calls 'unmotivated desires' – are desires (ends) that we just happen to have, that are simply upon us. However, the desires now under consideration, like desires for means, and the other desires that result from deliberation mentioned by Bernard Williams in the passage quoted on p. 3, would be the product of rational reflection. They would differ from the desires that result from deliberation on the basis of *already existing* desires for ends in that they would introduce entirely novel ends into the motivational system, ends *not* tied to the agent's already existing motivational set. I shall call these desires, supposing them to exist – and the only alternative is to deny the existence of external reasons – *reflective* desires, and their objects *reflective* ends. This will distinguish them from the desires (for ends) that are just upon us – the appetites and inclinations.

We may, in any case, conclude that every (standard) act is done to satisfy some desire of the agent, though not necessarily an appetite or inclination. There can be no action without desire. In that respect Hume was right. Having argued this, I wish now to go on to claim that it is a sufficient condition of an act's being *done for reasons* that it is done to satisfy a desire.

Most writers assume that an act is not done for reasons unless the agent sees something as a reason and acts accordingly. This is commonly called 'rational motivation', and is often supposed to take place only after deliberation. It is standardly assumed that explanations in terms of agents' reasons are only appropriate in cases of this kind. Sometimes all standard acts are supposed to be of this kind, sometimes standard acts that are not of this kind are relegated to an inferior class as somehow being sub-rational. I wish to say that whereas it is false that practical or deliberative rationality has a role in all standard acts (those done to satisfy a desire of the agent), all standard acts can nevertheless be said to be *done for reasons*, not just from an objective or third-person point of view, but from the point of view of the agent himself. Thus *reasons as motivating* are firmly tied to the intended satisfaction of desires as such.

To give a reason is to give an answer to the question 'Why?'. Since this question is often a request for an explanation, to give a reason is often to give an explanation. We speak, for example, of the reason why a pipe is leaking, the reason why water boils when it is heated, or the reason why birds fly south in winter. The reason in the first two cases, and arguably in the third, is a cause. We also ask why a person did what he did, which is a request for the person's *motive*. Now one can construe, or attempt to construe, motives as causes. But even if one does not, one can give an objective, third-person account of them. Here *the* reason for a person's act is simply the motive, however that is construed, and regardless of whether one supposes the matter of how the agent saw his own act and what it might achieve (relatively to his own desires in the context of the world as he saw it at the time) to be a necessary part of the explanation. But when we speak of *his* reason(s) we are necessarily considering how it was for him, and the account that the person himself would give of why he did what he did. Our paradigm act is, of course, one that is consciously directed towards a consciously desired end, and it is only where there is such conscious awareness of one's desired ends that practical reasons can gain a foothold. An act whose motivation was *unconscious* would not be a standard act. Nor would one whose real explanation *lay outside* the agent's conscious desires and beliefs. I am simply assuming that the motivation for most acts is *not* opaque to the agent himself – that he does what he does for the very reasons that he thinks he does.

The sort of explanation that interests us, then, is explanation in terms of his or her reasons, of which the person is aware, and which involves that person's conscious desires and beliefs. And we must be careful to maintain the contrast between this internal or *intentional* kind of explanation, and a third-person or objective explanation even if, unlike a behaviouristic or mechanistic explanation, it accepts the agent's intentional state as being essential. Thus *the* reason (the motive) for your running out of the building was that you *thought* it was on fire. I invoke your belief in giving the explanation. But *your* reason for running out of the building, *from your point of view at the time of the action,* was *that* the building was on fire. And this is a true intentional description of your motivation whether or not the building was in fact on fire. The third-person explanation invokes beliefs (propositional attitudes); the first-person (intentional) explanation, i.e. the explanation from the point of view of the agent as he or she saw it (his or her reason) invokes belief *contents* (the objects of the propositional attitudes) (cf. Bond 1974[1]: 336–7). Nevertheless it is often appropriate to use the very same language to describe the reason from the first-person (intentional) and third-person (objective) views, as the following taxonomy of motivation will show.

(1) We may begin with an act done from *simple inclination*, which is the limiting case of a standard act, hence of an act done for reasons. In such cases, the correct response to the question 'Why did you do it?', which is a request for a reason, is 'Because I felt like it', or 'Because I wanted to'. Here we can say that *the* reason (the motive) was simple inclination and that the *agent's* reason was simple inclination. It might look as if giving this answer to the question constituted or implied a *denial* that there was a reason. The agent might reply, 'I didn't do it for any reason at all; I just felt like

[1] I regard much of the content of this paper as superseded by the present work.

doing it.' But what is clearly meant here is that the action was not done towards any further *end*, that it was done for its own sake. A request for a reason ('Why?') can sometimes be a request to specify the *end* towards which the action was directed, and the answer to the question so understood will be given in an 'in order to...' formulation. In the present sort of case no such answer can be given, since the act was done for its own sake. But the reason *as explaining* need not be given in an 'in order to...' formulation. In fact, such a formulation *only* specifies the end-in-view, the desire for which may itself stand in need of explanation. Where the reason is explanatory, however, it may be true that the agent's reason *was* simple inclination, i.e. that he or she just felt like it.

(2) The second kind of act done for a reason, is an act done out of a certain *emotion*. In answer to the question, 'Why did you do it?' ('What made you do it?'), the correct answer may be 'I was angry' or 'I was afraid' or 'I was jealous'. The 'in order to...' formulation in such cases (that specifying the end-in-view) might be 'in order to hurt him' or 'in order to get away' or 'in order to remove him from the scene'. In such cases it is the emotion which explains the desire for the end. And again *the* reason (the motive) is the emotion, while his or her reason is also the (felt) emotion which includes, significantly, elements of belief. If the correct first-person account were 'I was angry because he hit me and I wanted to hit him back', the *strictly correct* third person account would be that he was angry because he believed (as it happened, correctly) that the other person hit him (on purpose) and, as a consequence, he felt a desire to hit him back. So a divergence between first-person (intentional) and third-person (objective) accounts exists even at this level, and that is because of the greater importance of the element of belief. But this distinction is not usually made in practice because in many cases, not without justification, it is *assumed* that the agent is not mistaken in his beliefs.

(3) The third category is that of *unwilled desires or aversions* (of which the desires of the first category are, strictly speaking, a subset), including appetites. These include all inclinations towards or away from (aversions) which, unlike simple inclinations, involve the desire for an end other than the action itself. These, together with simple inclinations, and the desires that are explained by emotions (Category 2), constitute Nagel's 'unmotivated desires', the desires that, as he says, 'simply assail us', or 'simply come to us'

17

(Nagel 1970: 29). Normally they are *felt* desires or aversions. In the simplest case (excluding simple inclination), the answer to the question 'Why?' would be 'Because I was hungry' or 'Because I was thirsty', and in general the first-person explanation would specify the unwilled inclination or appetite that the agent acted to satisfy. The 'in order to . . .' account would, in such cases, be of the form, 'in order to satisfy the desire which I feel (felt) for *E*' an 'in order to . . .' account that specifies it as an end desired for its own sake, and hence which does explain the act, provided there is no difficulty in understanding how the thing is a thing that *can* be desired for its own sake.[2]

The reason (the motive) in such cases is a felt appetite or aversion plus the belief that the act is a means to its satisfaction. The *agent's* reason is of the form 'I feel a desire for *E* and this is a means to its satisfaction', e.g. 'I am hungry and this is food', though, of course, the belief need not be, and normally is not, *articulated* by the agent. But just 'hunger' will do, in normal circumstances as an explanation from either point of view.

(4) The fourth category of motivation by reasons is where the agent consciously sees his act or its end as desirable, good, or worth having, getting, or doing under some aspect, including the useful (effective means to desired end). This is the sort of case where an agent consciously sees himself, upon reflection, to have a reason for doing something, and acts upon that reason. It is because the act is *seen as valuable* or desirable in some respect that it is done. It is here, and here only, that deliberative rationality can have a place in the explanation of an act, for it is here only that the motivation can be, even partly, the consequence of conscious reflection. It is here only that it is appropriate to speak of rational motivation. Yet, as we have seen, it is *not* the only kind of action that an agent does for reasons, even where reasons are construed intentionally, that is from within the agent's outlook on the world.

It is by considering this sort of case only that so many either assume or conclude that reasons tied to value or worth and reasons tied to motivation and hence to explanation, are one and the same. But it is only in this sort of case that they even have a meeting ground. *It is a sufficient condition of an act's being done for an agent's*

---

[2]There must be some aspect under which it can be understood as an object of desire. Note that this does *not* mean that the object must be characterized as *desirable* (good) in some respect. (see pp. 45–9 below.)

reason that there be a desire and a belief that the act constitutes (Category 1), or is a means to (Categories 2 and 3), its satisfaction. The agent, even when doing something for a reason, may not act for what he *regards* as a reason. An agent's acting for what he takes to be a reason, thinks is a reason, i.e. in order to gain some valued object, is the defining characteristic of Category 4 motivation.

Let us look at some of these kinds of value by examining some possible answers to the question 'Why?' which belong in this category. These may include:

  (i) 'It was the most efficient and least burdensome way to obtain *E*, my desired end.' (usefulness, utility)
  (ii) 'It was something I like doing.' (pleasure)
  (iii) 'Someone might have been hurt if I had not done it.' (prevention of harm to others)
  (iv) 'It was the only morally right thing to do.' (moral rectitude)
  (v) 'Because it would protect me from certain dangers in the future, it was in my own long-range interest to do it.' (prudence, self-interest)
  (vi) 'Not to do it would have been treachery, betrayal.' (fidelity, loyalty)
  (vii) 'It would have been base and ignoble to do it.' (personal virtue *per se*)

The corresponding 'in order to . . .' accounts would be:

  (i) 'In order to achieve *E*, which I desire.'
  (ii) 'In order to have fun (enjoy myself).'
  (iii) 'In order to prevent someone's getting hurt.'
  (iv) 'In order that right be done.'
  (v) 'In order to promote (protect) my interests.'
  (vi) 'In order to avoid treachery and betrayal.'
  (vii) 'In order to preserve (promote) my virtue (worth, goodness).'

Although only the first of these specifies the end as desired, the others are all understandable as possible objects of desire, in that they are all capable of being valued as ends of action. Though some (e.g. Bernard Williams) might want to hold valuations to be simply a subset of the desires that constitute an agent's motivational set, i.e. to regard them as essentially affective, we must consider the possibility that they may be essentially cognitive, that they are beliefs (to the effect that something, because it possesses some character, is valuable, desirable, or worthwhile) that are true or false, and which *generate* desires to seek the ends in question; that they are, in other words, reflective desires, as these have just been defined (pp. 14–15 above). In any case, we can distinguish these valuations, which are at least partly dependent upon reflection, from the appetites and aversions of Category 3, which are given quite independently of conscious reflection, and we must not assume that behind every one of these motivationally effective valuations, some such inclinational desire or aversion must lie.

The first kind of valuation illustrated, however, namely the recognition of the value of utility, the recognition that something is an effective means to a desired end, has a special character of its own. And that is because something is said to have value *as a means*, regardless of the nature of the end, so long as that end is desired. Those who, like Harman (1977), or Mackie (1977), would deny that value, considered as an *end*, can be cognized, would not deny the discovery or cognition of *utility*. Here is a cognized value, all right, but the value is derived from the presupposition that the end is in fact desired, and this fact of desire is enough, given that the means is effective, to establish that it has this value. But in all the other cases, it is the *end* that is supposed to be desirable or valuable as possessing a certain character. And it is difficult to see how this desirability can be reduced to *de facto* desire (see chapters 2 and 3).

The motivating reasons so far discussed either spell out or clearly imply the desired end. But what we call his or her reason may be a belief content (that *p*) relating the action, as means, to a desired end, whether that end belongs in Category 2 (desires arising from emotions), 3 (appetites or inclinations), or 4 (desires related to valuations involving beliefs arising from reflection), without either specifying or clearly implying, except contextually, that end. This is generally a straightforward factual belief. Thus my reason for moving quickly is that there is a bus bearing down on me, my reason for sending her flowers in the hospital is that it would cheer her up, my reason for giving up smoking is that smoking increases one's chances of having a heart attack by a factor of 10, my reason for telephoning is that I promised to, my reason for running out of the building is that it is on fire. All of these are factual belief contents which we have no difficulty in tying, contextually, to an agent's understandable desires.

Since reasons of this latter kind are all reasons because they are *seen as means* to desired ends, we may well ask whether they do not therefore all fall into Category 4, the category of actions on the basis of reflective desires deriving from valuations. But consider the following. Sometimes instantly, and without the need for reflection, one perceives something as a means to a desired end. Thus, for example, I might notice a bus bearing down on me and jump instantly out of the way. If someone asks me, 'Why did you move so quickly?', my answer will be that there was a bus bearing down on me. That, indeed, was my reason for moving quickly out of the way. Nevertheless we cannot say, in such a situation, that the agent deliberated, or even reflected (though he did perceive); indeed if he had taken the time to deliberate or reflect, he would probably not be alive to tell the tale. This is not an example of deliberative rationality, nor even, in the sense in which I use the expression, of rational motivation, i.e. motivation by considered reasons (though it is plainly an example of a rational act). The point is that *considered reasons* have played no part in the motivation, which belongs in Category 3, the desire being my inclination (instinct) to avoid what immediately threatens death, harm, or injury. But sometimes we come to believe that something is a means, or the best or most efficient means, to a desired end, after deliberation or reflection, and, as a consequence, desire it. And an act so motivated *is*, in my sense, a rationally motivated act, belonging to Category 4.

I have argued that it is a sufficient condition of an act's being *done for reasons*, even when this is construed intentionally, i.e. as his or her reasons, that it is done to satisfy some desire. And to this one need add only that it is a necessary condition of an act's being done to satisfy some desire that it (the act) be seen either as consisting in, or as being a means to, the end desired. There is no need to suppose that, to do something for a reason, an agent need act on the basis of what he or she *takes to be* or *sees as* a reason; that is only *one kind* of doing things for reasons, albeit a very important kind. We must now ask how all this relates to the vexed question whether reasons can be construed as causes.

First, we must consider just what the status of a reason is in the kind of explanation by reasons we have been considering. Donald Davidson, in his famous and much discussed paper, 'Actions, Reasons, and Causes' (1962), takes a reason to be a belief plus a desire. Others have variously seen desires or beliefs or both to be the ingredients of reasons, and the question has then been considered whether such things can be causes. What all such views have in common, however, is that they look at the action from a third-person or observer's point of view; they attempt to consider the question *objectively* even if they regard the agent's intentional state as an essential part of the explanation. But if I am right, the essential explanation is not an observer's explanation but one seen from the point of view of the agent, and from *that* point of view, both in Category 4 cases, and in those Category 2 and 3 cases where the act is seen as a means to the desired end, the reason is never a *belief* but always a belief-content, a proposition, something of the form 'that *p*', which is the object of a propositional attitude or what is sometimes called an 'intentional object'. In Category 1 cases, where the reason is always 'I felt like it', and simple Category 2 and Category 3 cases, where the reason is just 'I was angry', 'I was jealous', 'I was afraid', 'I was hungry', or something of the kind, where the belief content is minimal and the reason is simply given in a statement of one's emotional or orectic state, the reference is to the state *as it is felt*, to how it is to *be* in that state when one is oneself the subject.

There are two necessary ingredients in an explanation by agent's reasons, a thing (or things) believed and an end (or ends) desired. The reason is sometimes given in a statement of the content(s) of the agent's belief(s), either explicitly or implicitly tied to a desire, or in a statement by the agent of his orectic state, or of an emotional state which (in the context) accounts for the desire. But these things are to be understood *as they are for the subject*, for it is only as such that they explain. We understand the act by understanding how it was (or is) for the person as a conscious subject–agent.

What I wish to claim is that none of the things that can count as reasons, viewed intentionally – and that is the kind we are interested in – have the right *ontological status* to be causes. And that is because they have *no objective being at all*. They exist only as objects of thought (belief-contents, propositions), or as states of subjects (felt desires, felt emotions). One cannot raise *this* objection to *beliefs* (propositional attitudes) as causes, or even to desires or emotions as causes, because all of these can be construed in an objective, observer's, or third-person way, but then so construed these are *not* reasons or at least not *agent's* reasons, and it is explanation in terms of agent's reasons with which we are concerned.

Thus one may attempt to construe beliefs dispositionally, or as states of the central nervous system, or both, and, in the latter case at least, they might be regarded as causes, but one cannot so construe belief *contents*. Yet it is the belief *content*, not the belief, that is the reason, when a reason of this kind is construed intentionally, as it must be if our explanation is to be an agent's reason(s) explanation. And while there is a serious problem about desires, since they cannot be identified independently of their ends, one might also attempt to construe desire and emotions behaviouristically, or in physicalistic terms, or both, but desires and emotions *as states of a subject* cannot be so construed, yet it is desires and emotions *so understood* that have the explaining role where the explanation is an agent's reason(s) explanation.

Thus I conclude that reasons are not causes and that explanations in terms of an agent's reasons are not causal explanations. And note I do *not* have to invoke anything (either objectively or intentionally) normative or evaluative about reasons to make this claim. It is not a necessary condition of an act being done for reasons, in the relevant sense, that the agent act on the basis of what, upon reflection, he *sees as* a reason, and it is only that sort of case that would even appear to necessitate his having value beliefs, let alone whether those beliefs have any foundation. Motivating reasons, as I see them, even construed as agent's reasons, need not even contain a valuational element let alone an objectively normative one. Nor have I argued that reasons cannot be causes on the ground that the action and its alleged cause are internally related and cannot be identified independently of one another. So none of that controversy is germane to the point I wish to make, namely that reasons, being either propositional contents, which are intentional objects, or subjective states, or both, have *no objective or independent existence*. They exist wholly within the intentional world of the subject who thinks or feels them. Hence they cannot qualify as causes, since causes must have an independent existence as events. Yet if it is a standard act that is to be explained, it is an explanation in terms of agent's reasons that must be given.

Standard acts are not caused, they are *done*, by conscious subject–agents, for reasons. Chisholm (1966) and Richard Taylor (1966) are surely right in holding that agency, *doing*, is the *sine qua non* of (standard) action, and no merely caused event or occurrence for the explanation of which no agency is required, can be one. Causal explanations that would eliminate agency cannot be explanations of acts. There is no need to introduce any technicalities about 'agentcasuality'. It is simply that there cannot be a (standard) act without some agent bringing something about for the sake of some end which he or she has.

One possibility is that there are no acts, strictly speaking, or agents either, for that matter, but only occurrences, in current jargon that talk of acts and agents belongs to 'folk psychology'. This is, indeed, a strict consequence of physicalistic and some behaviouristic accounts of behaviour, but it is a view so strange that one can, without irrationality, choose to ignore it. That we do act, and for reasons, is far more certain than any theory that entails the contrary, however plausible its metaphysical foundations. Another seeming consequence of such a view is that there is no such thing as practical rationality (choosing for the best), and that is surely not a view that any sane person would be prepared to accept. Even B. F. Skinner, in *Beyond Freedom and Dignity* (1971), recommends (in effect) that we take certain measures in order to bring about certain desirable ends.

One thing, however, is quite certain. An agent will not do a thing if he has no motive for doing it, i.e. unless he desires it as an end or sees it as a means to the achievement of some further desired end. There is no 'freedom of the will' to do what one has no desire to do! Though no desire can *cause* an action, no agent can act except to satisfy a desire, so if there is no desire to be satisfied, no action can take place. Further, if an agent has a possible motive (i.e. a desire) to do only one thing, and no possible motive (i.e. no desire) not to do it or to do some other thing then, of necessity, he will do it. But (a) there is no need to suppose that this is *causal* necessity, nor (b) is there anything mysterious about it. It is trivially true that a person will not do what he has no possible motive for doing, and in the sort of case under consideration, there is only one thing that he has any possible motive for doing! Hence that is what, of necessity, he will do. It would be most misleading to say, in this case, that he cannot help but do it, as if he were deprived of freedom or choice, being somehow bound in the chains of necessity! It is not that he *can* do nothing else (poor sod!) but that he *will* do nothing else simply because he has no possible (motivating) reason to. Freedom of the will is not arbitrary: one will act only where there is desire. But this is not to say or imply that the desire is the cause. An agent of necessity acts to satisfy a desire, but if there is more than one desire, he may act on any one of them. One might suppose that he

24

necessarily acted to satisfy the strongest of his desires, but on examination this claim turns out to be empty or trivial, since the only criterion for a desire being strongest is that it is, in fact, acted upon. If we look for an independent criterion of strength of desire, on the other hand, such as how powerfully felt or close or urgent it is, it is not difficult to find examples of courage, heroism, or commitment to principle – even commitment to rational prudence – where such desires are overcome for the sake of what is regarded as a greater good.

Nor is there any implication here that acts are somehow mysterious or inexplicable. Suppose for purposes of argument that what I say is true, and that where there are two or more desires (possible motives), an agent may act to satisfy either one of them. If he chooses act A, in order to satisfy desire D_1, then his act can be quite adequately explained by this desire (provided it is an understandable desire), and his belief that A consisted in or was a means to its satisfaction. If, on the other hand, he chooses act B, in order to satisfy desire D_2, then his act is equally adequately explained by his having D_2 and his belief that B consists in or is a means to its satisfaction. Each is a perfectly adequate explanation for someone's *doing* something, though *not* in terms of causally sufficient conditions.

To the question, Why did he do A *rather than* B? (or *vice versa*), there are various possible answers. He may have reasoned that the end of D_1 was more worth while than the end of D_2 and acted accordingly. He may have reasoned similarly, but done B *in spite of* his value belief, because he was more powerfully inclined that way and suffered from *akrasia*. He may simply have done the one or the other because it occurred to him first. He may have tossed a coin. The answer will not be the same in every case. But whatever the answer, agency, not causal factors exclusively, must be involved. Otherwise we are not dealing with an act but with a mere happening, with which the supposed doer of the deed, as conscious subject–agent, had nothing whatever to do.

One must be very careful in talking about *the will* here. The mere use of the expression is likely to lead to a charge of faculty psychology, or worse, of harbouring a conception of volitions as mental events with physical effects. But I think one can speak safely of will as whatever is fundamental to doing and of *the* will as the power of agency. It is the idea of agency that is fundamental, and the concept of will is explained in terms of it, rather than *vice versa*. We do not introduce the will, or volitions, in order to account for agency – the latter notoriously will not do the job in any case – but we may speak of will, nevertheless, as the non-causal, agency-related *sine qua non* of something's being *done* as opposed to its merely happening. However there can be no will without desire.

As to the metaphysical difficulties – do not acts entail physical occurrences, and are not all physical occurrences deducible from the state of the physical world plus some law or set of laws and hence quite independent of the will? – I could not even begin to try to deal with them here. Certainly it cannot be the case that every act constitutes an interference in the laws of nature! Suffice it to say that it is more reasonable to believe that we are agents, that we do things, consciously, for reasons of which we are aware, than it is to accept any metaphysical or psychological or sociological theory which would require us to deny these immediate home truths. The metaphysical problem is there undoubtedly, and clearly there must be some solution, though at present I frankly confess that I do not know what it is. I know that agency is possible because it exists, but I do not know *how* it is possible. Notice, however, that there is no reference in anything I have said to *the mind* as an entity, or to *mental* events or occurrences as having any independent ontological status. I have spoken only of conscious agents, subjects, belief contents (propositions as intentional objects), and subjective states (emotions and desires as felt by a subject), all of which are involved in the explanation of acts in terms of agent's reasons. I believe it a serious error – one might call it the Cartesian fallacy – to reify, in the sense of construing as objects in the same world as physical things, the mind or the mental. While I am not, and cannot be, a materialist, I am most emphatically not a dualist either.

2

Motivating reasons and grounding reasons

My aim in this chapter is, first of all, to show that a distinction must be drawn between reasons that motivate actions and reasons that ground them, and further that this distinction is required to be drawn even if it is held that the satisfaction of present desires is the only ultimate ground for action. In the course of the discussion, I attempt to clarify the confusion surrounding the concepts of an irrational and of a rational act. I then proceed to argue that grounds for action are internally tied, not to desire, but to value or worth conceived quite independently of desire (value or worth which is not internally related to desire). Contra Bernard Williams *et al.*, external reasons, i.e. reasons not tied to any member of my present motivational set, can and do exist. Further, these do not derive their character as reasons from an internal relation to the agent's future desires (Foot and Nagel) or, for that matter, to the desires of others (Nagel).

In the case of both value-specifying reasons of Category 4, and factual belief-contents tied to desires of Categories 2, 3, or 4, it is the belief *content* (the *object* of the propositional attitude) that is the reason (his or her reason) when that reason is viewed internally (intentionally) from the point of view of the agent. If this *is* the explanation of the act, then, the third-person observer (objective) account will include a reference to the agent's beliefs or belief states. Belief states (propositional attitudes) figure in the third-person (objective) explanation. In neither case, however, is the truth value of what is believed relevant to the explanation. We are not concerned, where explanation is what we are after, with anything beyond the belief states (third-person explanations) or the intentional world (first-person explanations) of the agent.

To return to an earlier example. Someone believes that the building he is in is on fire and, as a consequence, he leaves. His motive is to save himself; the relevant desire is the felt aversion to whatever threatens death, pain or injury. His reason for leaving the building, construed intentionally (as he sees it), is that the building is on fire. The explanation of his leaving is his belief that the building is on fire, together with his felt aversion to what causes death, pain, or injury, and his belief that fire is such a cause. *The reason he left was that he believed (rightly or wrongly) that the building was on fire.* Viewed objectively, it is true that he left because he believed the building was on fire, regardless of whether the building was on fire or not. Viewed intentionally, *that* the building was on fire was his reason, even if in fact, it was not on fire at all.

But if the building was *not* on fire, then the agent did not *have* a reason or at least did not have *this* reason (the reason he thought he had) for leaving the building. The reason on the basis of which he acted was not a reason he *had*. Thus one can act *for* a reason that, in some sense, one does not actually have. And from this it follows that the sort of reasons one *has* (in this sense) and the sort of reasons that motivate (the reasons *for which* one acts) cannot be the same. *The sort of reason that motivates is entirely related to the intentional world of the agent. The sort of reason an agent actually has is connected to the world of facts beyond the agent's beliefs.* I can leave *for* the reason that the building is on fire – and that is the correct intentional description whether the building is on fire or not – but (in a sense) I cannot *have* that reason unless it really is on fire. Since we clearly have two sorts of reason here, let us call the first kind *motivating* or explaining reasons, and the second kind justifying or *grounding* reasons. It is these latter that specify or contextually imply whatever is to be accomplished or gained (desire to be satisfied, good to be obtained or whatever) by the performance of the act. *And note that we are required to make this distinction even if we hold that all reasons, of whatever kind, must be tied to actual, present desires.* For suppose my reason (intentional) for doing A is that it will bring about desired end E, but in fact doing A will not bring about E. Then the reason for which I act is a reason that I do not actually have.

Is it *irrational* to leave the building because it is on fire when in fact it is not? It is not irrational if one's belief, though false, is well grounded. If one has *good reason to believe* that the building is on fire, then it is irrational not to leave. Thus, paradoxically, an act or abstention can be *irrational* if it is *not* done for a reason that does *not* exist, and (equivalently) rational only if it is done for that non-existent reason. In such cases, however, one does indeed have a reason to leave, though not the reason one thinks one has, and that is the real possibility or likelihood, as determined by the evidence, that the building is on fire. So this is not, *per impossibile*, a case of an agent's being irrational for failing to act when *no* reason exists.

However, if the belief is ungrounded, neurotic, or delusory, i.e. if there is no reason (no grounds) for believing that the building is or might be on fire, then it *is* irrational to leave. Indeed this is a paradigm of an irrational act. Where one's deeds are dependent upon beliefs, when the beliefs are irrational the deeds are too. So an act can be irrational even if it is rationally motivated, in my sense. (He believes, irrationally, that the building is on fire, and acts for – as he conceives it – that reason.) Thus a rationally motivated act need not be rational. This common view is nothing but a muddle.

Akrasia (weakness of will), which is another kind of irrationality, also consists in doing something irrational for a reason. Here the agent's *beliefs* may be perfectly rational, yet he fails to do what he himself believes he has the best or most reason(s) for doing, and acts instead for some reason (usually tied to a present appetite or inclination) which, as a grounding reason, he consciously acknowledges to be lesser or inferior.

In the present example, the agent thinks he has a reason and acts *for* that reason (so conceived), even though he does not actually *have* it. But there are also cases of acting for reasons, e.g. because one feels like it, to satisfy an appetite, because one feels an emotion (instances from Categories 1, 2, and 3) where thinking one has a reason plays no part in the motivation at all. Here the agent does not see his act as grounded or justified, nor does he even consider what is to be achieved by it; he simply acts upon the inclinations which he feels. Here there are *only* motivating reasons: there is not even something which is *seen* as a grounding reason. Yet such acts can be perfectly *rational*, that is to say not irrational or contrary to reason, even though they are not *rationally motivated,* as I use that expression, i.e. in the sense of being done on the basis of considered reasons.

Unfortunately the expression 'rational act' is sometimes used, confusingly, to mean 'rationally motivated act', and yet again to mean 'rationally *grounded* act'. Thus 'rational act' has (at least) a threefold ambiguity. Its primary sense seems to be the complement of 'irrational', that is to say a person is acting rationally so long as he is not acting irrationally, i.e. doing what is stupid, senseless, or crazy. It is in this sense that, as I just said, an act can be rational even if not rationally motivated. I have also just pointed out that, though rationally motivated, an act may be irrational. Since the truth conditions of these two concepts of a rational act, namely (1) not irrational, (2) rationally motivated, are completely independent of one another, the ambiguity is a most unfortunate one.

A rationally *motivated* act is one done on the basis of what one *takes to be* a reason; such an act is rationally *grounded* when one is not mistaken in one's belief, i.e. when one really has the reason one thinks one has. Obviously an act can be 'rational' in the sense of 'rationally motivated' when it is not rational in the sense of 'rationally grounded'. A fourth possible sense of 'rational act' is 'rationally *justified* act', i.e. where a reason or reasons not only exist(s), but is (are) sufficient to determine that the act is, all things considered, one to do or to have done. Much philosophical discussion of reason as it relates to action is vitiated by these ambiguities. It will be best to reserve 'rational' for the primary sense ('not irrational'), and to use the expressions 'rationally motivated', 'rationally grounded', and 'rationally justified', whenever these are meant.

It is only in cases where one supposes oneself to have a reason and acts for that reason, so construed, that deliberative rationality can gain a foothold. But in all cases, including cases of this type, reasons as *motivating* (reasons *for which* a person *does* something) are reasons because they are tied to the agent's subjective system of desires, beliefs, and emotions, whereas reasons as grounding (reasons for and against doing a thing) are tied to the world beyond. It must at least be the case that the means *will* achieve the desired end, or that the object *is* of the kind supposed, or that, where the motivating reason is a factual belief content, that the belief in question is *true*. Otherwise the agent only supposes he has a reason which in fact he does not have.

We must accept the following paradox. An agent can act *for* a reason, so understood, which nevertheless he does not *have*. The only way to resolve the paradox is to distinguish between (1) the reason, so understood, *for which* he acts, namely that p (construed intentionally), and (2) the reason, the *fact* that *p* (construed objectively), which he only thinks he has. The first, what is *seen as* a grounding reason, is his motivating reason; the second is the grounding reason, which he *has*, which *exists*, only if his belief is true. In cases of this kind, grounding reasons are facts, while motivating reasons are belief contents only.

Deliberative rationality succeeds only where (a) the agent is acting on a reason he supposes he has and (b) he really does have it. (This is only a necessary, not a sufficient condition, since there may be other and better reasons for doing otherwise.) For neither of these conditions can 'reason' be understood as 'motivating reason', for that can exist regardless of the state of the world beyond the agent's subjective (intentional) state, yet the reason he supposes he has and must indeed have, is tied to truths in the world beyond that state.

We are now in a position to refute the suggestion, mooted on pp. 4–5, that the apparent internal connection between having reasons, and values achievable by action, be severed or denied. If the motivating desire is in Category 1, then thinking one has a reason plays no part in the motivation. If it plays a part in the motivation when the motivating desire is in Category 2 or 3, that is because the act is seen *as a means* to the satisfaction of the desire, and that is to see it as possessing *instrumental value*. And if the desire is in Category 4, then it is, *by hypothesis*, reflectively regarded as possessing value or worth. Thus we can conclude that when we act because we believe we have a reason, our belief is a belief that something of value or worth, whether instrumental or intrinsic, lies in the performance of the act. This leaves open the possibility that we do not regard the end we desire as possessing worth when we value an act as a means to its accomplishment. But that does no damage to the position I want to advocate. My claim is that we cannot see ourselves as *having a reason* for acting without *ipso facto* seeing our act as valuable or worthwhile in some respect, and instrumental value, which is concerned only with means, *is* a species of value. Thus we may conclude that the reasons we think we have (and may indeed have) are grounding reasons and that they are internally tied to values.

As we have seen, there is one and just one kind of motivation by reasons where practical rationality and deliberation may enter, namely that of Category 4, where we act on the basis of valuation, after reflection, either of ends as possessing certain desirable

31

attributes or of our actions as means to desired ends (instrumental value). In such cases one acts for something that, as a consequence of reflection (present or previous), one *takes to be,* regards as, or accepts as a reason for doing something, though one may be mistaken.

According to Bernard Williams, (1979: 18–19), there are just two ways in which one can be mistaken: (1) one can identify something as a desired object when it is not, or (2) one can suppose something to be a means to a desired end when it is not. Actually having reasons, as distinct from thinking one has them, on Williams' account, is still tied to what he calls a person's 'subjective motivational set'. What I am calling 'grounding' reasons must, on this account, be tied to a person's actual desires or present set of motivational propensities. Basically, according to Williams, one has a reason for doing something if it will satisfy some desire which is a member of one's actual motivational set, where that desire is not based on a false belief. There are no *external* reasons, i.e. alleged reasons that do not satisfy this condition. But why should this be so?

A reason, to be a reason, it is argued, must be capable of figuring in deliberation as a possible ground or basis for action, and hence provide a possible motive, but one deliberates on the basis of one's actually existing motivational set. Hence no alleged external reason, since *ex hypothesi* these are *not* tied to one's motivational set, can figure this way in deliberation, and thus no such alleged reason can motivate. And so a reason, to be a reason, *must* be tied to an actually existing desire or motivational propensity.

The only alternative to this would be the kind of externalism of reasons with respect to motivation advocated by David Richards (1971). Reasons exist and may even be recognized as reasons, yet, in the absence of the relevant desire, may fail to have any motivational force or influence. Richards denies even that reasons are tied to values which, according to him, belong in the sphere of motivation. But if reasons are not tied to values and, even if recognized, have no motivational power, by what right do we call them 'reasons'? What can we *mean* by calling them reasons. One might also advocate maintaining the connection between reasons and *values* while denying the connection between the recognition of values achievable by action, hence the recognition of reasons, and motivation. But this would only create an additional problem about what could be meant by describing a possible end of action as 'valuable' or 'desirable'. Surely Williams is right in this regard, and it is senseless to say of someone that he acknowledges something as a reason if he is not, to some extent, motivated towards doing the thing for which the reason is believed to be a reason. And how can this be so if he does not desire the end, whatever it may be?

Gilbert Harman argues, on similar grounds, for the impossibility of a rationally grounded universal morality (1977: 107–10), as does Rodger Beehler (1978: 137–43). One can have a reason for doing something only if one already desires the end which the act serves to accomplish. Thus only people who desire the ends of (a) morality have reason to be moral. Moral reasons do not apply to all rational agents. And this is also a clear consequence of Bernard Williams' view that reasons, for an agent, must be tied to his already existing desires.

Is this the choice that must be made, then – between an externalism that, because all connection with motivation has been severed, leaves us in doubt as to what might be meant by 'having reasons', and the view that reasons exist for a person only if he already has the relevant desires, a view that would make any objective values, including moral values, impossible? It is certainly the choice that Williams and Harman think is forced upon us. Nor, as we have seen, does Nagel show us the way between the horns of this dilemma: for cognitions cannot, *per se*, motivate, nor can 'desires' that are the mere logical ghosts of actions.

What is true in the Williams–Harman–Beehler position, is that if a reason is to count as a reason in deliberation, it must be tied to a desire, that is if the deliberation is to result in action, and that, after all, is its point. In this sense, internalism is true. One cannot acknowledge something as a reason in one's deliberations without this having *some* motivational force, and it can only have *that* if it is tied to a desire. But, and here is the crux of the matter, a reason *can exist* without its being recognized or acknowledged as a reason, or without the agent's being aware of it at all. And this is so when there is something to be *gained* by the agent by doing the thing in question, something that he himself, were he aware of it, would recognize as possessing value or worth.

Bernard Williams (1979: 21–3) cites the example of Henry James's Owen Wingrave. Whereas Owen is completely unmotivated towards the military life, and his father knows it, the father urges that *there is a reason* for him to join the army, namely that it is a family tradition and family pride requires it. As Williams says: 'The whole point of external reason statements is that they can be true independently of the agent's motivations.' Further, Williams grants that if Owen were to come to believe this, i.e. come to accept that this reason exists, then he *would* have the required motivational propensity: 'The agent does not presently believe the external statement. If he comes to believe it, he will be motivated to act; so coming to believe it must, essentially, involve acquiring a new motivation. How can that be?' (1979: 23).

What Williams perforce denies is that coming to believe the external reasons statement, i.e. coming to acknowledge that the reason exists, can be an act of understanding or *cognition* purely, which is what the 'external reasons theorist' must hold, since only then could the reason be said to exist prior to its acknowledgement. (If it were only a change of *affect* then it could not accurately be described as coming to acknowledge a reason that already existed, but the reason the existence of which one now acknowledged would have *come into being* with the change of affect.) He denies it by claiming that the statement that an external reason exists amounts to or entails the claim that, if the agent rationally deliberated, he would come to be motivated to do the thing in question, or to have some motivational propensity to do it. For if this were *not* entailed, the connection with motivation would have been severed. By hypothesis, the supposed external reason is not tied to one's existing motivation, yet one can *deliberate* only on the basis of one's already existing desires (since only then can the deliberation result in action). So there can be no true external reason statements, hence no external reasons.

The flaw in this argument lies in the claim that an external reasons statement must be equivalent to or entail the statement that if the agent deliberates rationally he will acquire some motivation to do the thing in question. This merely begs the question, since the whole point of holding that reasons may exist for an agent independently of his motivational system (that there are external reasons) is that the agent may not be *aware* of the thing that possesses the value or worth which determines that a reason for action exists, or he may not be aware that it possesses that worth. What we come to believe in coming to believe an external reasons statement is that something of value or worth is to be achieved by the action in question, and *this* is what the statement means. Of course if the

34

agent does not *recognize* this worth, and if he lacks any other possible motivation for doing it, then no amount of deliberation will create any motivation to do it. Nevertheless the reasons exists, in virtue of what is to be *gained* by doing the thing, whether the agent is aware of it, and hence can use it in his deliberations, or not.

This also shows why an agent is not necessarily irrational in failing to act on a reason which does exist for him, and which outweighs any contrary reasons, when that reason is purely external (i.e. tied to a genuine value unknown to or unrecognized by the agent). Not knowing that the reason exists, he cannot take account of it in his deliberations. Hence it can hardly be irrational for him not to act on it. *Contra* Bernard Williams, the 'external reasons theorist' need not be construed as claiming that the agent who fails to act on an external reason, when it outweighs any contrary reasons, is irrational. The agent's fault is not irrationality but ignorance.

By contrast with the Owen Wingrave case, consider the following example. I know someone who has been exposed to a little classical music but not very much. He has never heard any Brahms and thinks he would not like it. Knowing what I do about his still only partly formed tastes, I have a hunch that he would like Brahms very much, starting with the First Symphony. And suppose my hunch is correct. A reason exists, therefore, for his going to a concert where this work is being performed, or for listening to it on the radio, or for buying a recording of it. The reason is *that he would enjoy it,* or *that he would find it very beautiful and moving,* or *that hearing it would prove very worth while.* (We hesitate to say that *he has* a reason just precisely because he is not aware of it and hence cannot make use of it.) The reason has nothing whatever to do with his present system of motivations. Nevertheless it exists. It is, therefore, an external reason, in Williams' sense.

It might be argued that he has a desire to hear music that he likes, or which will please him or, still more generally, that he has a desire for pleasing experiences. Hence the reason for his going to the concert *is* related to his present desires. But we are speaking here not of the object or objects of desire *in general* (the desirable, the enjoyable, or whatever). These matters are discussed in the next chapter. (See especially p. 44 below.) We are speaking, rather, of desires for specific objects. What matters in the present context is that no deliberation on the basis of his present desires (including their general objects) and his present knowledge could result in a desire to go to the concert, unless he does it in order to please me or to keep me quiet. The reason in question is a reason that exists yet, being unknown to or unrecognized by the agent, *cannot motivate*, hence an external reason in the relevant sense.

In order to please me, the person goes to the concert and he *does* find it worth while. He *discovers* its value. A new desire enters his motivational set – the desire to hear Brahms' First Symphony on appropriate occasions – and another new desire, to hear more works of this composer. However these *desires* are not what give him reasons for future auditions of Brahms – those reasons would exist even without the desires – but rather the prospect of enjoyment, the likelihood of gaining a certain benefit, the probability of gaining what is good, valuable or worthwhile. A reason that actually exists must be tied to a *potential* member of an agent's motivational set but not to an actual member, nor to one derivable from already existing members by deliberation. The discovery of value *generates* desire, as the example above clearly illustrates. It can introduce wholly new factors into an agent's motivational set. The recognition or acknowledgement that a reason exists, a necessary consequence of which is that one has some motivation to perform the act in question, *can* be the discovery or recognition of previously unrecognized value.

Let me repeat: the future discovery of as yet undiscovered value will cause new desires to enter an agent's motivational set. But this does not mean that there being present reasons not tied to an agent's existing motivational set (i.e. external reasons) is a consequence of those future desires rather than of the values generated by their discovery. This, if true, would be sufficient to overturn Williams' claim that there are no external reasons. Nagel, for instance, claims that reasons tied to my future desires but to none of my present ones can act as present rational motivators. (Hence the possibility of prudence.) But this is not what I am saying at all. I am saying that there may exist a value that actually provides now, and possibly in respect of my present or immediate good, an external reason, but one that cannot provide any motivation because it remains unknown and unsuspected. Indeed, *contra* Nagel, I deny that there *can* be any motivation without real, live, present desire. (Logical ghosts are not enough.) In that respect I am in complete accord with Williams.

A reason may actually exist for a person though he or she cannot be motivated to act on it because it is unrecognized. What makes a reason a reason, therefore, cannot be any present desire, since no relevant desire may exist. But neither is it any future desire. For what provides the reason – in the Brahms case the future possibility of aesthetic appreciation and its associated pleasure – need not involve, at least initially, the satisfaction of a desire. There need have been no prior desire for an object of that kind; the valuable object may simply have been stumbled upon. And the fact that this discovery generates future desires for more of the same has no part in determining that the object possesses value. Rather the value is constituted by the presence of appreciable aesthetic qualities and the pleasure of their apprehension. Hence, the fact that the discovery of the value generates future desires has no part in determining the existence of a grounding reason for seeking the object.

Should any doubt remain, consider the following example. I may be so constituted that a certain sexual caress will bring me undreamed-of ecstasy. It follows that a reason exists for my seeking it. If I am fortunate I may encounter this joy or discover it in the course of sexual experimentation, and this will generate future desires for it. But I may die without ever having discovered this value, and without ever having any suspicion of this particular susceptibility of mine. The value, hence the reason, existed all along for me, yet no desire for it ever existed or, *ex hypothesi*, could have existed, since the object remained unknown.

My position is not to be confused with the position that, in addition to present desires, future desires (Foot and Nagel) and the desires of others (Nagel) can provide reasons. I am making the much stronger claim that the existence of grounding reasons (though not of motivating reasons) has no internal or necessary connection with desires of any kind.[1]

The main difference between Bernard Williams' Owen Wingrave

[1]For further examples illustrating the independence of (grounding) reasons from desires, see Grice 1967: 10–12 and 16–17. The example (pp. 16–17) of the unsuccessful actor who wants nothing but to be an actor but who would, in fact, be successful and happy in another career, perhaps best serves my present point, but all the examples are germane. (Grice reserves the word 'reason' for grounding reasons alone. Where I speak of 'motivating reasons' or 'explaining reasons', he speaks of 'motives'. My way of speaking would seem to be closer to daily discourse, since by 'reason' we may mean either the one or the other or sometimes, confusedly, both.)

example and my example of the developing music lover is that whereas listening to Brahms is a good for the latter even before he is aware that it is, James makes it clear that there is nothing of value for Owen in joining the military. Although it is in theory possible that Owen, or someone like him, might, after having been forced into it against his will, find the military life completely enjoyable and fulfilling, it is unlikely, and James, as author, can stack the cards heavily against it. In this respect the Owen Wingrave example is tendentious. However there is still something to be learned from it. Wingrave senior is strongly committed to the values of family tradition and honour, values which he takes to be universal, and in declaring that a reason exists for Owen to join the military, though it is unrelated to his present desires, he is declaring, in effect, that such universal values exist and hence reasons exist that are reasons for everyone relevantly circumstanced, Owen included. Owen denies, in effect, that these are universal values by denying that they are values for him, hence that he has this reason for joining the military.

Notice an important difference between this and the case of the developing music-lover. Some people are tone-deaf; there are others who are not tone-deaf but are nevertheless constitutionally unable to appreciate Brahms. No one would wish to claim that they, in spite of their desires, had any reason to listen to Brahms. The reasons why my developing music-lover should listen to Brahms are external in that they are not tied to any of his present desires, and furthermore they are universal in the relevant sense, in spite of the fact that they are dependent upon his capacities for appreciation. This is so because, like the claims respecting family honour, they are understood as reasons for anyone similarly circumstanced, the circumstance in the present case being the capacity to appreciate Brahms. If one has no family tradition or honour to uphold, one cannot have this reason for doing anything and, if one lacks the capacity for appreciating Brahms, one cannot have that reason for doing anything. But given these conditions, the reasons exist and are universal.

There is, however, an important difference. The developing music-lover's reasons relate to his own personal good (even when they are not tied to his present desires); the act is to be done, if you like for the agent's own good. But in the Wingrave case, Wingrave senior is best understood to be claiming that these are values which exist and which should motivate us, *regardless of,* or *in spite of,* our own personal good. One should, if necessary, *sacrifice* one's own personal good for the sake of the values in question. Wingrave senior is saying, in effect, that considerations of family tradition and honour create a *moral obligation* on Owen's part to join the military. Now if there is such a thing as moral obligation, it must not be based upon considerations – I shall not bother to rehearse the well-known arguments – of the agent's own good. However, that moral obligation is created by considerations of family tradition and honour is a highly dubious proposition. If, on the other hand, Wingrave senior is saying that family honour and tradition are part of Owen's own personal good, it is quite right to reject the suggestion. There is nothing in it for Owen at all. But notice that the existence of a reason is here denied, not because family traditions and honour are unrelated to Owen's present or future *desires,* but because they can have no *value* for him.

We saw in the Brahms case that someone can come to have a desire for a thing, hence a possible motivating reason for seeking it, as a consequence of an *encounter* with value, and the *promise* of further reward. The value was there for him all along, hence there was a reason all along for him to listen to Brahms, but a reason he could not act upon until he became aware of it as a reason, which he did only when he actually discovered the value of Brahms' music by listening to it. But this direct encounter is not the only way he might have come to believe in the value of Brahms' music. It may be that whenever I have recommended a certain piece of music or a certain composer to him in the past he always found it or him enjoyable or worthwhile. If I then proceed to recommend Brahms, he may believe on *inductive* grounds that Brahms will prove worth listening to. As a consequence he will believe that he has a reason for listening to this work and, as a consequence of that, he will have a possible motive for doing so. Coming to believe that something is desirable or worthwhile (worth having or getting or doing), even on inductive grounds, generates in an agent a desire for it and hence some motivational propensity towards it.

Suppose he does listen to Brahms' First Symphony for either of these reasons: (1) that the work has proven enjoyable in the past, or (2) he believes me when I tell him he will enjoy it. Generalizing, we can see that this is the sort of case where A does x for reason R because he reflectively sees R as a reason for doing x. R specifying or

39

implying (often contextually) what there is of worth to be gained by doing x. This – the motivating reason is in Category 4 – is, as I said, the only sort of case where practical rationality can gain a foothold, i.e. to some extent determine choice. In such cases we can say that the grounding reason, construed intentionally, i.e. as the agent sees it, is one and the same with the motivating reason, construed intentionally. As the agent sees it, R is a reason (specifying or implying the value to be gained), and he consciously acts for that reason (in order to obtain that thing of worth). The reason is, throughout *the same belief-content*.

It is through this identity of grounding and motivating reasons, when both are understood intentionally, or from the agent's point of view, that deliberation and practical reasoning can succeed, that rational motivation is possible. Of course this identity does not guarantee success. One may act on such a reason construed intentionally when no such reason, construed objectively, exists. There is an actual grounding reason only when what is believed to be worth having, getting, or doing, really is worth having, getting, or doing. Of course what one believes, in believing that one has a grounding reason, is that something *is* to be gained (including losses retrieved, and evils overcome, lessened or avoided) by the performance of the act. But such beliefs often prove false. Actual or objective grounding reasons, as providing rational grounds for action, are logically tied to value, i.e. to what, among ends achievable by action, are really valuable desirable, or good – are genuinely worth having, getting, or doing. It is the aim of deliberative rationality to achieve what is most valuable or worthwhile in a particular situation, to choose the sort of action best supported by reasons, or supported by the best reasons (the most important values), to do what one should do or what one ought to do, to do what is right or best. Hence deliberative rationality is internally or necessarily tied to value.

The entire picture should by now have become clear. On the one hand, there is a conceptual connection between grounding reasons and values achievable by action (what is worth having, getting, or doing) and, on the other hand, between motivating reasons and desires or wants (motivational propensities). The confusion between the two kinds of reasons leads to the supposition that somehow grounding reasons must be tied to wants, and this error is reinforced by the existence of the kind of case, discussed above – the only kind of case where deliberative rationality comes into play – where what the agent *sees as* a grounding reason (grounding reason construed intentionally) becomes one and the same with the reason why, looked at from her point of view, the agent does what she does (motivating reason construed intentionally). But, as we have seen, this does not mean that the grounding reason, *construed objectively*, must be tied to the agent's desires or wants; rather it is tied to what is worth having or getting or doing, given her circumstances whether she is aware of it or not. In this respect all grounding reasons can be seen, in a sense, as external reasons, since they are reasons not in respect of being tied to the agent's desires (or motivational set), but to goods achievable by action which ground or justify that action or determine, *ceteris paribus*, that it ought to be done. They *become* internal or motivating reasons (though not the only kind) upon recognition of the value as a value (hence the reason as a reason). One cannot believe something achievable by one's action to be worth having, getting, or doing, without as a consequence, having some motivational propensity towards it.

There is, as the non-cognitivists suppose, a necessary connection between valuing and desiring, but the connection is not one of identity, necessary or contingent. In coming to recognize that a possible end has worth, I at the same time conceive a desire for that end, but this is a desire that is *explained* by my belief, which is the product of reflection. It is not the case *either* that the desire–belief pops into being, or that the belief is a shadowy logical consequence of a quite spontaneous desire. For, without the reflection, the desire could never be. Indeed this is how such desires are distinguished from the appetites and inclinations 'that simply come to us' of Categories 1, and 3, and the relevantly similar desires of Category 2.

3

Desire and the good

I hope I have argued persuasively (1) that grounding reasons must be distinguished from motivating reasons, (2) that, unlike motivating reasons, grounding reasons are tied to goods achievable by action rather than to desires, and (3) that grounding reasons get into the motivational system when they are *recognized*, i.e. when it is known what value an action has or will achieve. And if this is correct, we are no longer required to see grounding reasons as necessarily tied (in order to motivate) to the agent's already existing set of desires or motivational propensities. Nor may one suppose that this is because some reasons are internally tied to the agent's future desires or to the desires of others. Grounding reasons are not internally tied to desires of any kind.

However one could still hold, compatibly with this but on other grounds (or no grounds at all), that value simply *was*, in fact, the object of desire, and that value or good for an agent was achieved if and only if some desire of his was satisfied. Thus there could be a grounding reason for doing something when and only when doing it would satisfy some desire of the agent, value consisting essentially in just that.

Note that this is not identical to the Williams position, which depends upon a supposed internal relation of grounding reasons to present desires, nor to the positions of Foot or Nagel, who insist upon an internal relation to desires of some kind or other. Further, Williams' position is perfectly compatible with the denial of any internal connection between grounding reasons and values and, indeed, neither Williams nor Nagel need be construed as saying anything about *value* at all.

The present view, that value is nothing but the object of desire, gains support from the fact (cf. p. 20 above) that, in the case of utility or efficiency, it is a sufficient condition of an act's possessing that value that it be an efficient means to some desired end, leaving completely aside the end's worth. But in every other case it is the worth of the end that is in question. The theory under discussion holds that an end's merely being desired is a sufficient condition of its worth for the desirer. It is, in fact, a very common view, one often taken as self-evident and seldom argued for. There are various desired ends, it is assumed, and there are means to their achievement. The value of the end is simply left unquestioned. The desire *confers* it.

One should not confuse this view that desire *confers* value on its ends, with the, in some respects, very similar view, that there is *nothing but* desire and its objects, that there is no axiology but only psychology, or that the so-called theory of value must be reduced to motivation theory. As I understand it, this latter is the view of Nagel in *The Possibility of Altruism*.

The view that value just is the object of desire could be extended to include not only present, but also future desires. Indeed it is a common view, perhaps best expressed by Rawls (1971: 399–411), that my overall good consists in devising and acting upon a 'rational life plan' that will enable me to satisfy as many and frustrate as few as possible of my own desires over my lifetime, with preference being given, in cases of conflict, to the satisfaction of the greater over the lesser (or the frustration of the lesser over the greater) desires. A person's good consists, in other words, in a rationally-ordered economy of want-satisfactions over a lifetime, what Rawls, somewhat confusingly, calls 'goodness as rationality'. A presupposition of this view is that every desire-satisfaction is of itself inherently good, and if it is not rational to satisfy a desire, that is only because it will prevent the satisfaction of more or greater ones. Rational prudence (the pursuit of one's own good) just is the working out and actual pursuit of a lifetime economy of want-satisfactions. Value, on such a view, is a function of desire-satisfaction, and failure to get what one wants is the only evil.

Any such view will, of course, have to accommodate any case (cf. the Brahms example, pp. 35–6) where we discover something new that delights us or is otherwise found to be valuable not as a means but as an end, and where it seems right to say that this end, since it was not even known, could not have been desired prior to the discovery of its worth. And there are also cases where it seems right to say that a thing, while previously within one's cognizance, was not desired *until* it was recognized to have worth as an end, this state (of having worth) existing prior to the recognition of it and

43

hence prior to the desire, so that it was a good for the agent even before he desired it. Thus the company of a person long scorned may turn out, on further acquaintance, to be uniquely valuable, contrary to all expectations, and I may deeply regret the attitude that kept his company from me for so long. Examples of this kind certainly make it appear that desiring a thing is not a *necessary* condition of its possessing worth for an agent. Nor does it seem, on the face of it, to be a *sufficient* condition, for what one has long desired may prove empty or worthless when one gets it at last.

Against the claim that desiring something is not a necessary condition of its having worth, one might try to argue for some sort of necessary connection between a thing's proving valuable and its being desired, such that if a thing proved valuable it would *have* to be true that it was desired. But what sort of a necessary connection might this be? It certainly does not *follow logically*. We could *stipulate* that if something proved agreeable or otherwise valuable, then it was something desired. But it would still not be desired in anything other than the stipulated sense of 'desired', and that would amount to no more than saying that it proved valuable. We could try saying: we all desire whatever has value for us, so if a thing has value for us, it is something desired. But the point of the counter-examples is that we might not have known that it (or things of that kind) had value for us, if we knew about its existence at all, hence *it* (or things of that kind) was not desired. In any case, 'We all desire what has value for us' only has the appearance of necessity of it is construed intentionally rather than objectively. But construed intentionally it means we desire whatever we *see as* having value for us, which is not something I would wish to deny; indeed I want to say that the perception of value achievable by action *generates* a desire for it. But the point of the counter-examples is that the thing we found to have value or worth was not previously perceived to have that worth, and hence could not have been desired on those grounds. And the same would go for 'We all desire what is agreeable', 'We all desire what gives pleasure', and so forth.

What I shall call the '"really want" dodge' has been used against both the claim that desiring a thing is not a necessary condition of its proving valuable and the claim that it is not a sufficient condition. If a thing is discovered to have value, then that shows it was what one 'really wanted', and if one wants something but is disappointed when one gets it, that shows that one did not 'really want' it. But it is plain that 'really want' here is simply being used as a synonym for 'liking' or 'finding good' or 'being satisfied with'. And 'really wanting' a thing in this sense does not require any *actual desire* for the thing before it is obtained. One only 'really wants' what one is satisfied with, and being pleased with a thing is a sufficient condition of 'really wanting' it. 'Really wanting' is not a species of wanting or desiring at all. The pleasure or felt satisfaction is the real source of the value, not the supposed wanting.

Another dodge, one used by Rawls (1971: 416–17), is what I call the '"what one would want if one knew" dodge'. But this one really does give the show away. It is not what he or she *actually* wants, given their present inadequate knowledge, that determines what possesses value for an agent, but what she or he *would* want, *if* they knew (perhaps with the aid of Scrooge's ghosts) what the consequences would be like for all of the choices open to them, that is if they were able to *sample* the consequences of all of the choices open to them. But, of course, if one were able to sample the possible outcomes, then one would know *from experience* what they were like; one would know which ones were satisfying and which ones were not, and one would, *as a consequence*, reflectively desire only the satisfying ones. But this makes it plain that the value lies in the potential felt satisfaction, not in the desiring. One reflectively desires the things one does because one has *discovered* their value. One desires *because* of the value; the value does not exist because of the desire.

An ambiguity in the words 'satisfy' and 'satisfaction' also lends support to the view that what is good is whatever is desired, a good that is gained by having the desire satisfied. In one sense of 'satisfy', it is a sufficient condition of one's *desire* being satisfied that one *gets* what one wants; if you get what you want, then (it follows) your want is satisfied. But it does not follow from this that *you* are satisfied in the sense that you derive any pleasure or satisfaction, now in the other sense of *felt* satisfaction, from the acquisition, since it may yield no reward at all. One could argue that value lay in satisfactions, in this second sense – this would be a form of hedonism – but these felt satisfactions would not be a necessary consequence of the satisfaction of desire.

This is not to say, of course, that there could be satisfaction without desire. That there be a desire that in fact has been satisfied is a (conceptually) necessary condition of satisfaction of any kind. Felt satisfaction is simply pleasure in the desired object now obtained. Coming to possess a desired object does not always produce felt satisfaction – the object may turn out to be bitter or disagreeable or worthless – but sometimes it does, and the value thus yielded is hedonic. Not all hedonic value, however, consists in satisfactions of this kind, for a pleasant or enjoyable object may be encountered serendipitously, without any prior desire either for it or for anything of its kind. Still, this form of restricted hedonism would have more plausibility than any attempt to identify the realization of value for a person with the satisfaction of her desires *simpliciter*, i.e. with desire satisfaction in the first sense.

One is forced to conclude that where value has been discovered a desire exists, but the thing is not good because it is the object of desire – one may desire something when one mistakenly believes it to have value – but because of its actual proven worth. And it will *possess* this worth whether or not it has been discovered, for it cannot be *discovered* if it does not already exist. So it is not desire-satisfactions or desire-frustrations *per se*, that have positive or negative value, but things such as likes and dislikes, joys and sorrows, pleasure (delight) and unpleasantness, satisfactions (in the second sense), benefits, rewards, and goods of all kinds, including non-self-regarding goods, as when we acknowledge another person's good as a value for us to pursue. Practical rationality aims at these things, not at desire-satisfactions *per se*, or an economy thereof. That is not where value is located.[1]

If we take the Williams position, as stated, and combine it with the view (which Williams might well wish to deny) that grounding reasons (the reasons that one actually *has*) are internally tied to values, we can derive the following.

One *has* a reason for doing A, hence there is a value for the agent to be gained by doing A, if and only if it is a means to the satisfaction of some desire, and that desire is not based on a false belief (e.g. wrongly supposing something to be a means to a further desired end, or wrongly identifying a thing as being of a kind desired).

It would follow that the satisfaction of any desire not founded upon a false belief, and this alone, was a contribution to an agent's good.

[1] Of course what is *needed*, as distinct from what is wanted, is, of necessity, genuinely valuable. For a discussion of needs, whose objects are certain instrumental goods the absence of which are evils, see p. 131 below.

But, as the illustrations here and in the last chapter have shown, a good may exist for an agent prior to his discovery of it or his belief in its existence, and hence prior to his desiring it (if he ever does come to discover or believe in it). Further, the satisfaction of a desire, even when there is no false belief as to the nature of the desired object (excepting that it is supposed to possess some value) or as to the efficacy of something as a means, may prove worthless when it comes. In connection with the first point, we must consider not only such things as the value of Brahms for someone capable of appreciating him but who has not yet discovered his music, and the unrealized ecstasy of the unexperienced sexual caress, but also the just mentioned serendipitous realisation of some value or good – an interesting encounter with a stranger, a play of light and shadows, arriving at the crest of a hill and finding a breathtaking prospect – where desire and its satisfaction, even the generation of future desires, seem to have no place at all. For in none of these cases have we found a new desirable end to be sought; rather we must just take these things as they come.

This (revised Williams) position should be compared with Elizabeth Anscombe's claim that one may be mistaken in supposing that a desired object possesses a certain desirable character (in virtue of which it is desired), but not in supposing that character itself to be desirable, since that must be one of the real forms of good (1957: 75–6). That a character which an object is supposed to possess is desired is a guarantee of its desirability or worth. Thus if the desired object turns out not to possess the worth it was supposed to have, that can only be because it lacks the character in respect of which it was supposed to be desirable. For Anscombe too, that an object is desired, hence (on her view) seen as desirable under a certain aspect, is a sufficient condition of its goodness, provided the object does possess the aspect in question. But this leads us to consider one possibility in respect of the revised Williams position that has been overlooked.

We might consider that a desire for an end is founded on a false belief if its satisfaction (first sense) will not in fact give any satisfaction (second sense) or other reward, benefit, or good. The implication here is that it is a necessary condition of desiring a thing that one believes it to possess value; desiring is necessarily for the desirable, intentionally construed. Without a belief in the desirability of the end, a belief which may be false, a desire cannot exist. The desire is wholly dependent on the desirability belief. Thus all desire contains a cognitive element as part of its essence. 'Desire is for the desirable' expresses a necessary intentional truth. So if the object of a desire proves undesirable, that shows that it was founded on a false belief. There is no need, at this point, to go all the way with Anscombe and claim, in respect of the *character* possessed by the object thought desirable, that desire cannot err. On the present proposed view, the error may be either that the object lacks the character it was supposed to have, or that that character itself was erroneously thought to be desirable.

The revised Williams formula becomes: One has a reason for doing A (and this implies that there is something to be gained by doing A) if and only if it is a means to the satisfaction of desire D, and the satisfaction of D will result in such satisfaction or other benefit as is necessarily anticipated in desiring it. Note that all reasons, on this account, would be 'internal' reasons, in Bernard Williams' sense, though no desire could exist without a belief that its satisfaction would pay off in some way or other, and there would be no grounding reason if this belief were false. Thus reasons, while fully 'internal', i.e. tied to actual desires, would nevertheless also be firmly tied to actual worth, profit, benefit or other good.

This is only going to work, however, on the assumption that desire is, of necessity, intentionally for the good; that, of necessity, we desire only what we believe to be good (desirable) or to have worth, that such a belief is a necessary condition of desire, that necessarily we desire a thing in respect of seeing it as desirable under some aspect of character. This is a view argued for at length by Anscombe (1957: 66–77). It seems further to imply that the value belief is the source of the motivation. This is plainly true where the belief is a belief that a certain act is an effective *means* to the accomplishment of a desired end, where the value lies in this efficiency. For the desire to perform the act in question will be wholly dependent on this belief (together with the desire for the end). But where *ends* are concerned, the doctrine would imply that every one of them belonged in Category 4, the category of valuation, where, in respect of things valued as ends, an agent does something *because* he sees the action as being or bringing about something thought of as worth having, getting, or doing for itself (as an end) under some aspect. And if my account of motivation by desires in chapter 1 is anywhere near the truth, this is simply not so.

There are desires (appetites, inclinations, emotion-determined propensities) which, as Nagel puts it, 'simply come to us', and which we are not moved to act on by a reflective consideration of what good they will bring. But perhaps it might still be true that we can only desire a thing if it is seen as desirable under some aspect, though the belief is not itself the *source* of the desire. Let us consider some of the wants other than the reflection-dependent wants of Category 4 (evaluations).

In the case of Category 1, pure inclination, where the person's reason is that he or she just feels like doing it, there is plainly no conception of the thing as good under any description; it is a case of pure impulse. *Is* there a reason for acting on such impulses? Perhaps. It may be good for you sometimes to act on pure impulse. But when I act on pure impulse it is not on the basis of this consideration, or indeed on the basis of any consideration, that I act. The motivating reason in that case would be, 'Because I feel like doing it and doing what you feel like doing is good for you' and that is *not* doing something just because you feel like it! In any actual case of action upon pure inclination, I do not act upon a reason which I believe I have. I do not even consider whether there is a reason for doing it or not. I do not need to see my act as good under any aspect. I just do it because I am so inclined. (Remember that this is a case where I act *for* a reason, though whether I actually have a reason *or* think I have a reason is totally irrelevant.) And if the satisfaction of my desire does not pay off (yield pleasure or felt satisfaction), that cannot be because I falsely believed the object of my desire to be good.

In the case of Category 2, desires stemming from emotions, one of my examples was hitting someone back because I am angered at his hitting me. The answer to the question, 'Why did you do it?' is 'I was angry and I wanted to hit him back.' There is no question of my seeing my act as good or desirable under any aspect, or of this playing any part in my motivation. Hence if I derive no felt satisfaction from hitting him, that cannot be because my desire is founded on a false belief. (Compare this reply to the question with 'I wanted to give him what he deserved' or 'I wanted to stop him from going around hitting people.' These, by contrast, are Category 4 motivations, where, provided this *is* the correct account of the motivation, I act after some reflection and for the sake of some (as I see it) good.)

In Category 3, consider the case of pure appetite. Thirst is upon me, and so I drink something which I take to be water, or at least fluid that will satisfy this appetite. Several things are clear: (1) The appetite itself – desire for water or other thirst-satisfying fluid – is not the product of any reflective beliefs and is in no way dependent upon them. (2) My desire for this particular bit of fluid *is* dependent upon my belief that it is the sort of thing that my appetite is an appetite for. (3) I may misidentify the fluid as water when it is, say, rubbing alcohol; in which case, if I start to drink it, I shall quickly recognize it as not being the object of my desire. But that this kind of false belief would rule out an agent's actually having a reason was part of the original Williams position. Having a reason (or there being a value) is ruled out because the desired end is *not achieved*. The kind of false belief we are concerned with here is belief that a desired end will satisfy when in fact it will not. And the present example, since drinking rubbing alcohol was *not* the desired end, is not an instance of that. To have a desire for a certain object, one is required to believe that the object desired is of the *kind* desired, but one is not required to believe that *if* it is of that kind, then it will bring satisfaction, other than in the sense that one will have got what one wanted, and that does not, as we have seen, imply that one received felt satisfaction or any other benefit. Unlike rubbing alcohol, a soft drink, or even salt water may answer to one's desire and reinforce it; but it may taste terrible and may not (in the case of salt water will not) even quench one's thirst. In the case of appetite, there is no need to believe that *its* object is good in any respect, hence when its *satisfaction* (sense 1) does not pay off we are not entitled to say that the desire was founded on a false belief in the object's worth, and that *that* was why its object did not have value.

It is true, as a matter of fact, that the satisfaction (sense 1) of appetites, both natural and induced (e.g. drug addiction) normally brings pleasure (as well as relief). That is why it is natural in this context to speak of gratification rather than mere satisfaction. And thus, as a matter of fact, a person who has an appetite upon him, usually anticipates pleasure in its satisfaction. But there is no necessity here. Some orgasms are disappointing; all of them *could* be. But even if they were *and we knew it*, this would have no effect on sexual appetite, which would be *upon* us as much as ever. And while on the subject of sex, compare a man or woman who makes love because he or she has an appetite for it, and a man or woman who wants to have the pleasures of sex and, lacking the appetite, takes what he or she believes to be aphrodisiacs, in order to *induce* it. The second is an instance of Category 4 motivation. Sex is *thought good*, conceived on reflection to be desirable, and what are presumed to be means for achieving the valuable object are taken. In the first case the people are simply moved to act by their appetites; they need not give the matter any thought at all.

Besides it is as plain in the case of appetites as it is in all other cases, that the value lies not in a thing's being the object of desire, but in the reward or benefit or good that it accomplishes or brings when it is achieved. Though the gratification of an appetite normally brings pleasure, this is an empirical matter that is, in the case of the natural appetites, easily explained in biological terms. There is no necessity here. Nor does this imply a Benthamite view of pleasure as something distinct from and caused by the activities, sensations, and other experiences that are said to be enjoyed. When a thirsty man enjoys his drink, his pleasure is a felt quality of the experience of drinking the water, not logically separable from that experience, and hence not caused by it. But if thirst *just is* the desire to drink water, for an appetite cannot be identified independently of its object, and the pleasure is *in*, not caused by, the drinking of the water, so that drinking the water is inherently pleasant, then is not thirst and, by extrapolation, any appetite, a desire for what is inherently pleasant, so that its satisfaction *logically* guarantees pleasure? If this were so, then if one did not enjoy an experience, then no appetite *could* have been satisfied, since an appetite is, of necessity, for something pleasurable. Among desires, appetites would, of necessity, not only be intentionally for a good, but for a good in reality as well.[2]

It is an ambiguity in 'Drinking water is inherently pleasant' that gives this argument its plausibility. *This* experience of drinking water, when thirsty, if it is pleasant, is inherently pleasant, but it does not follow from this that drinking water when thirsty is, *per se*, inherently pleasant. Yet the latter would have to be true for the argument to go through. It remains contingent that drinking water normally is, in these circumstances, inherently pleasurable. There is no necessity about this inherent pleasurability. One might add to this that putrid water may, while being extremely unpleasant to drink,

[2] This point was raised by Charles Taylor in a private conversation at Cambridge in 1979.

satisfy one's thirst, and distasteful food may satisfy one's hunger.[3]

One consideration remains. What of the *discomfort* that attends any unsatisfied appetite? Surely the satisfaction of an appetite of necessity removes that, so that having the appetite guarantees that its satisfaction will have at least this value? No, for as Hamlet noted, increase of appetite may grow by what it feeds on. The satisfaction of an appetite *can* not only not decrease or remove it, but may actually increase or reinforce it. Drinking salt water may satisfy one's desire to drink water, but it cannot slake one's thirst. There is no assurance, in acting to satisfy an appetite, that afterwards the appetite will go away, even temporarily. Nor need a person, in the grip of an appetite, necessarily think that it will.

The view we have just been considering is one that tries to establish an identity between what has value for an agent and the object of that agent's desires, by making good dependent on desire and by rejecting as a possible object of desire anything that yields no benefit when obtained. But, as we have now seen, it is false that every desire creates a value provided it is not founded on a false belief. On this present account it is clearly the object's *being* valuable independently of its being desired that is doing the work (cf. the 'dodges', pp. 44–5 above). But then why make desire a necessary condition at all?

The view does, however, permit error in the perception of value beyond just that of supposing something to possess a value-bearing quality when in fact it does not. On the present view one could value something, say accumulating money, as an end, only to conclude later that this was not a goal worth pursuing. In that case, if one's new judgment is correct, one's desire would have been founded on a false belief, namely that accumulating wealth *was* an end worth pursuing. Anscombe's view, however, does not permit this kind of error. We can be mistaken in supposing that an act or an object possesses some desirable character but not in supposing that character to be desirable. It must be one of the real forms of good. This statement stands isolated, undefended, as if its truth were self-evident (Anscombe 1957: 76). The following is certainly true: if desire is intentionally for the good, and this is an internal, hence necessary relation, then the object of desire will fail to be good only if there is some error of judgment. Now one way in which judgment can err is in supposing an object to possess some property

[3] I owe this last point to Stephen Nathanson.

or quality seen as value-bearing when in fact it does not. But why cannot one be mistaken in taking something to be a form of value? Why must a character one regards as valuable or desirable be valuable in reality?

One of the chief functions of Anscombe's 'desirability characterisations' is to explain a desire and hence a motivation. For, it is said, not just anything can be desired; one must know under what aspect the object of the action is seen as desirable by the agent before the desire, hence the motivation, can be understood. We must understand, as it were, what the agent sees as being *in* it for him before we can understand why he tried to get it. Now, if what I have argued so far is correct, this will be true only of cases where the end of an act is seen as valuable in some respect and is done as a consequence of being so seen (Category 4). It will not apply to the ends of Categories 1, 2, and 3, where value-beliefs play no part in the formation of the desire and hence no part in the motivation (though these things are done for reasons). But when the motivation is in Category 4, reflective motivation by what are taken to be reasons, then some sort of evaluation or value judgment is an essential part of the motivation. An act *of this kind* can only be explained if we know the characterization under which the agent sees the end as valuable – 'enjoyable', 'morally required', or whatever. Anscombe seems to think that all desires are of this kind, that we need a desirability characterization to explain any desire, hence any act at all. But, as we have seen, that is not true. We can *understand* someone's doing something on a sudden impulse (pure inclination), or to satisfy an appetite, or out of jealousy or fear *without* postulating any evaluation on the agent's part. And what we need, in order to explain an action, if the end *is* desired on the basis of an evaluation, is not one of the *real forms of good*, but something which can understandably be *taken to be* one of the real forms of good, i.e. which can understandably be regarded as good, valuable, or worthwhile. Nothing further is needed for the explantion to succeed. There is no need to introduce real or actual value in order to account for motivation. It is motivating reasons that are required (in this case reasons *seen as* grounding reasons), not grounding reasons, in order to account for motivation. This criticism seems to be reinforced by the fact that Anscombe, unlike many others, would not accept 'morally required' – a character that many *see as* desirable – as a real form of good (see Anscombe 1958).

It looks as if Anscombe has simply slipped from the intentional to the objective mode. Unless, of course, she *believes* that valuing a character, or a character's being regarded as valuable, is a sufficient condition of its *being* valuable. Many casually assume that what is valuable for a person or a society is what that person or society values or holds valuable, and Anscombe *may* be one of these, though I doubt it. It is, in any case, patently false. To value is to regard as valuable, and that is to regard a thing as valuable indeed, not to regard oneself as regarding it as valuable, and no such belief is incorrigible. Belief alone cannot create its objects; no more can valuing create value. The only alternative to this is to hold an 'error theory' of valuation, such as that advocated by Mackie (1977: 35, 48–9), according to which all value beliefs, since there are no objective values, are systematically false, and valuing something in reality amounts to no more than wanting it. But there are many good reasons, as I hope to have shown, for supposing this to be false. And besides, the price would be too great to pay. To value something as an end of action is to see oneself as having a reason for acting in order to keep, get, or do it, but one does not have this reason unless the thing really is worth having, getting, or doing. If valuing is really nothing but wanting, then deliberative rationality is a delusion. We would even have to abandon the notion that means-to-end efficiency had objectively determinable worth.

Anscombe may hold her position as a consequence of supposing, quite correctly, that a particular object of desire cannot falsely appear good, *tout court*; it must appear to possess some real *form* of good. ('"Good",' said Professor Anscombe in her 1978 seminar, 'is not the name of an appearance.'). But there are two ways in which a thing can falsely appear to possess some real form of good. It may, perhaps in virtue of lacking some natural property, not have the character, seen as valuable, which it is thought to have, *or* that character may not be valuable, contrary to what the agent believes. In neither case are we compelled to say that some particular thing is or appears to be good *simply*, rather than in virtue of possessing some character. Valuation aims at the good, but it is not incorrigible, even in respect of the characters or properties deemed to be good.

The person who believes that he has a reason to do something must *ipso facto* believe that there is something of value or worth to be gained by the action and, except in the case of instrumental value (the useful), he must understand the end of the action (possibly the action itself considered as an end) to be valuable or desirable under some aspect (e.g. noble, agreeable, pure, brave, beautiful, prudent, profitable, just, etc.) beyond its being *merely wanted*, since that does not specify what he thinks is *in* it that gives him a reason for doing it. And this desirability ascription may very well be culture-relative. But, I shall have to ague, for an agent to *have* a reason (as distinct from thinking he has one), the value in question must be one of the universal values for mankind, which follows from its *really being* a value as distinct from merely being *valued* by an individual or a culture. And this, I think, is the truth that Anscombe was really getting at when she said that the value-characterisation must be one of the real forms of good. It need not be; it need only be something understandably (perhaps only from within a certain culture) *thought* to be desirable. But if it *really is* desirable, hence *really does* provide a reason, then it *is*, of necessity, one of the real forms of good.

We may conclude that not all, but only reflective desires are, of their nature, even intentionally for the good. When we act on a reflective desire, we act for a reason we believe we have which, where the reason is tied to a valued end, is to act in order to achieve something we see as possessing worth or value. Valuing, or believing good is the source of reflective desire and, just as every belief aims at the truth, so valuing, where ends are concerned, aims at what is truly good, that is to say what is truly worth having, getting, or doing for its own sake. But as no belief is incorrigible, value beliefs too can be mistaken; not only may something turn out not to be a means to a desired end, but the end itself may turn out not to have the value or worth it was supposed to have. And all of this is in perfect accord with common sense.

The reason why so many philosophers, Williams, Mackie, Harman and Foot among them, seem so intent upon denying these home truths and, in the case of both Williams and Mackie, rejecting beliefs that are built into our very ways of thinking and speaking, is that they fear the ontological and epistemological difficulties that acceptance of the objectivity of values would get them into, Mackie in particular fearing commitment to a realist account which would have values forming part of the 'fabric of the universe'. On the other hand others, such as Wiggins and McDowell, see no objection to a realist or partly realist account of values (1976).[4] The account of values I wish to give is objective but not realist, but I shall save this discussion for the two chapters that follow.

In the meantime some general conclusions can now be stated. Desire or wanting is internally tied to motivation; motivating reasons are the reasons that one acts *for*, that explain one's acts. Any act done in order to satisfy a desire, i.e. any standard act, is one done for reasons, understood intentionally. But it does not follow from an act's having been done for reasons that the agent acted on the basis of *what he took to be* a reason or reasons. That applies to one kind of motivation only, namely where the desire is tied to a valuation, where the act is reflectively seen as desirable under some aspect, and done as a consequence. I call these desires *reflective* desires, and distinguish them from appetites, inclinations, and desires arising from emotions, all of which 'just come to us'. When an agent sees something as a reason, he sees it not as a motivating, but as a grounding reason, i.e. as tied to a value achievable by action. Reasons of this kind, to the extent that they actually exist and are not merely *thought* to exist, are tied to actual values or goods, to what is truly desirable or truly possesses worth, i.e. is worth having, getting or doing. It is in the case of this kind of motivation, namely Category 4 motivation or *rational* motivation, that deliberative rationality can enter the picture. Where rational motivation succeeds, what is *seen as* a grounding reason becomes one and the same with the motivating reason, also construed intentionally. That is how rational motivation is possible. Rational motivation succeeds, however, in the sense of achieving its end, only when the reason thought to be a reason really is a reason, that is when the end really is, as it is supposed to be, worth having, getting, or doing.

[4]The paper by John McDowell was read at a conference at Oxford in 1979.

4

Objective value – I

I hope I have succeeded in exposing as fallacies a number of commonly held views: (1) that one cannot draw a valid distinction between motivating and grounding reasons; (2) that reasons, to be reasons, must somehow be tied to wants (agent's present wants, agent's present and future wants, wants of all persons); (3) that there is no internal connection between reasons and values; (4) that desire creates value; (5) that there is an internal connection between desire and the desirable (the good) so that one can only desire what one regards as good (valuable); (6) that valuing creates value; (7) that an act done for reasons is always a rationally motivated act; (8) that a rationally motivated act is necessarily rational; (9) that an act done for reasons is necessarily rational.

The schema we have is as follows. (1) Motivating reasons, but not grounding reasons, are internally tied to desires. (2) Grounding reasons, but not motivating reasons, are internally tied to values. (Thus one has a reason for doing something if and only if there is something worthwhile to be gained by doing it, and one thinks one has a reason for doing something if and only if one thinks there is something worthwhile to be gained by doing it.) (3) Desire is only necessarily for the good (understood intentionally) in the case of reflective desire, i.e. where the desire is itself a product of (reflective) valuation. (4) In the case of rational motivation, i.e. action for what one regards as a reason, the reason one supposes oneself to have *becomes* the reason for which one acts. Thus, in such cases, the grounding reason, viewed intentionally, and the motivating reason, viewed intentionally, are one and the same reason. This is the meeting ground of the two kinds of reason and it is what makes deliberative rationality possible. (5) The union (as it were) of the two kinds of reason comes about when, as a consequence of seeing something, in respect of its having some character which one values, as a good achievable by action, one *desires* that thing and acts accordingly. Thus the reason as (supposed) grounding reason maintains its internal connection with worth, while *qua* motivating reason, it maintains its internal connection with desire, the *sine qua non* of action. (6) Nevertheless the grounding reason does not *exist*, hence the agent does not *have* it, unless the relevant factual beliefs are true and, except in the case of purely instrumental value, the end in question really is worthwhile. (7) It is neither a necessary nor a sufficient condition of the end's being worthwhile that it is in fact desired, even when the relevant factual beliefs are true.

Recall that this schema enables us to retain the Humean doctrine that there can be no action without desire, and that cognition (*contra* Nagel) cannot *qua* cognition determine the will; yet it permits us to say that cognition can determine the will, but indirectly, through the reflective desires created by the cognition of value. Nor is there anything strange or mysterious or incomprehensibly Platonic about this. In fact there is no reason why it should not be accepted, at least in respect of instrumental value, by everyone, even those who hold most tenaciously to the view that there is no question of the worth of an end beyond its being desired. For what is it to discover that something is an efficient means to a desired end other than to come to know that it possesses instrumental value? And this generates a reflective desire for the means as means, though it may be quite undesired – may even be an object of aversion – for itself. For those who hold that there can be no question of the value of an end beyond its being desired, or who would dismiss the value of ends as either non-existent or unrelated to deliberative rationality, deliberative rationality will be confined to deliberation about means plus the kind of combining, time-ordering etc., referred to by Bernard Williams in the passage quoted on p. 3. We will only be able to act in order to satisfy those desires that 'simply come to us', or such other desires as result from deliberation upon those desires. There is no room in such a scheme for the apprehension of values not tied to desires that already exist, no room for reflective desires other than those tied to means, to planning, combining, time-ordering, etc., and all of these are explained by reference to desires that 'simply come to us'. So far as ends are concerned, either (a) they are just wanted and nothing more, or (b) their value is entirely a function of their being wanted, the value being realized when the want is satisfied.

But both (a) and (b) have now been rejected, (a) because of the (now established) internal connection between reasons that one has (grounding reasons), including those one has in respect of ends, and values, and (b) because there is no escaping the conclusion that desiring an end is neither a necessary nor a sufficient condition of its actually possessing value for the person who wants it. Even with respect to personal pleasures, where the case for value being a function of wanting seems strongest, the proof of the pudding is in the eating. To have reason for pursuing something, when that reason is pleasure, it is not sufficient to want to do it, one must have *reason to believe*, either from having actually sampled the activity or experience in question, or on inductive grounds, that it will be enjoyable. It is the value (or the likelihood of its realization) that provides the reason, and it is the recognition or understanding of this value (or the likelihood of its realization) that brings the reason into the motivational system and makes it possible to act on it. It is the recognition, or the belief (whether well or ill founded) that produces the (reflective) desire, when the act is rationally motivated. (We must not forget that many acts done for reasons – in order to satisfy appetites, etc. – are not rationally motivated, i.e. not done on the basis of reasons one reflectively sees oneself as having.)

So desires for things that please us because we believe they will please us, are desires deriving from cognition, not, like natural appetites, desires 'that come to us'. It is true that the only reasons that can count for us as reasons in deliberation, are reasons tied to things we desire; otherwise these reasons could not motivate us. But one only *has* a reason if there is something to be gained by the action (something of value or worth to be achieved), and one only *sees oneself* as having a reason, hence one can only be motivated on the basis of seeing something as a reason, if one believes that something of value or worth is to be achieved by the action. And this is always a matter of belief, cognition, or understanding. If one sees something as a means to a desired end and, as a consequence, desires that thing, that is a desire which results from cognition or understanding. If we desire an end because we believe it will give us pleasure, that is a product of cognition or belief. That we simply *desire* a thing, however, cannot be construed by the desirer as a *reason* for pursuing it, since in merely noting that it is desired, no value has been specified, hence no reason has been given. (We know its being desired is not a sufficient condition of its having worth even if the desire is not based on a false belief.) Even if it were true that we could desire a thing *only* if we thought it to possess some value (a view disputed in the preceding chapter), it would be the possession of that value, or the likelihood of this, that provided the grounding reason and the belief that this was so that provided the *supposed* grounding, hence motivating reason, and not in either case the desire *per se*. Rational motivation is motivation based on the presumption of value. The desires on which a rationally motivated person acts are desires deriving from cognition, understanding, or belief.

On the view that would deny value to ends other than in respect of their being desired, the function of deliberation (practical reason) would appear only to be the selection of means, plus the time-ordering, etc., of the ungrounded or unmotivated (to use Nagel's expression) desires that we already have, desires that 'just come to us'. But we have now seen (a) that these desires cannot in themselves constitute or be the source of those reasons which an agent supposes himself to have when he acts on the basis of what he takes to be reasons, nor the source of that *kind* of motivation, i.e. rational motivation (although they can constitute or be the source of reasons for which a person acts when he or she is *not* rationally motivated), and (b) that many of the desires for ends on the basis of which an agent deliberates actually can provide reasons of this kind because they are desires *based on* or *deriving from* the understanding that something is worth having, getting, or doing it for its own sake. They are desires for ends that enter the motivational system *through* the agent's coming to understand or believe that these ends possess worth.

So far as personal pleasure is concerned – or, not to be unduly hedonistic, all that one finds or has reason for believing worthwhile *for oneself* – these discoveries or inductively grounded comings-to-believe are not themselves part of the deliberation process if by 'deliberation process' we understand trying to come to a decision, on the basis of reasons, what it is best to do in some particular situation. They nevertheless do constitute an input into the set or system of desires or motivations, based on either the apprehension of or intimations of value. Speaking loosely, they enter the motivational system through cognition, and that is the possibility that the 'internal reasons only' theorist is at such pains to deny. And let us remind ourselves once more that while such cognitions or beliefs *generate* desires, the reasons, if they exist, relate not to these desires but to the *values*, and it is because such reasons, hence values, are *thought* to exist, that the agent can be motivated rationally with respect to ends.

What pleases or interests me need not please or interest you. What I find worthwhile, you may find boring or tedious. These are commonplaces foolish and pointless to deny. Yet I have spoken even here of the *discovery* of value; desire cannot create value, even of this kind. I must *find out* what I like, what pleases me, what interests me, what is worth having, getting, or doing for myself. It is not a product of my desire or my will. Finding out that I like something will dispose me to seek it out, but that is another matter. The value, in such a case, is not a product of the desire, but rather the desire is itself generated by the discovery of value. Nor does the value lie in the satisfaction of desire *per se*. It is true that if I find I like something, I will desire it, and if my desire for it is then satisfied (provided I still like it), I will receive some satisfaction. But the value then lies in the enjoyment of the thing, not in the fact that some desire has been satisfied. (On this point, see my remarks on p. 45 above). Mackie (1977: 27) says that a value which consists in the satisfaction of desire is not an objective value. I agree. No value that is a function of desire, supposing there were such a thing (which there is not), would be an objective value. But that I like something, that it interests me, pleases me, satisfies me, occupies my talents, makes me feel good, etc., is not a product of my desires and must be discovered by me in the course of living. It is therefore *objective* relative to any pre-cognitive state of mine. It is not created from within; it is discovered in the world. I shall say that the value a thing has for one person but possibly not for another is objective but not common.[1]

Of course the thing that has this kind of value for some person has it in virtue of being (e.g.) enjoyable, satisfying, absorbing, relaxing,

[1]Some time after these chapters were written, Thomas Nagel kindly let me have, in advance of publication, photocopies of the corrected proofs of his Tanner Lectures given at Oxford in 1979 (1980). In the language he adopts there (following Derek Parfit), I can be construed as claiming that the value of these things is objective, but agent-relative rather than agent-neutral. But this language is taken by Nagel to apply to reasons and values only *in a general form*, i.e. to reasons and values (e.g. being pleasant, being in my interest) that are common. However I am speaking here of the realm of personal taste or preference, (which is pleasant, therefore good, for Smith but boring or unpleasant, therefore bad, for Jones), a realm which Nagel would seem to consign to the ineluctably subjective. (Nagel, unfortunately, continues to regard the object of desire as *eo ipso* a value for the desirer.)

and these *value-characteristics* are inherently valuable for all persons. And while objectivity does not imply being common, being common does imply objectivity. Further, the goodness or value that is inherent in such things as pleasure is very obviously not there as a consequence of my desiring or willing it to be there, nor as the consequence of my desiring or willing the things, i.e. pleasure, relaxation, etc., themselves. (On this point see also pp. 97–9 below.)

It will be recalled (chapter 2) that Bernard Williams has argued against the possibility of reasons existing outside the agent's already existing set of desires or motivational propensities by saying that if they did exist the agent would, upon deliberation, come to have the relevant motivational propensity, that he would be *irrational* if he did not act upon these reasons when there were no countervailing reasons, and that this could not be, since *ex hypothesi* these reasons are unconnected to his desires. 'Reasons' that cannot motivate cannot be reasons at all. My reply was that this begged the question since the whole point of the claim that there are 'external reasons', i.e. reasons not already having some motivational force, is that there may be things genuinely worth having, getting, or doing as ends for an agent, of which he is quite unaware, the reasons related to which gain their motivational force only when the agent comes to recognize them as worth having, getting, or doing. And, it seems I might have added, there is no need to suppose that these things can be discovered *by mere reflection*, or deliberation on the basis of what one *already* believes and wants, or by the exercise of pure reason or deduction.

This applies most obviously in the case of what I have called personal values, what is or would be rewarding or worthwhile *for ourselves*, as an activity or an experience or a way of life. For this really is a matter of discovery through experience; it requires living, not just thinking. Thus there might *be* a reason for someone (not necessarily Owen Wingrave) to join the military, in spite of his present strong aversion to it, because in fact, though he is quite unaware of it and would not believe it if it were told him, the military life would be more rewarding and profitable to him than any other life he could possibly choose. Contrary to his present beliefs, it could be just his dish of tea. And, of course, there is no way he could discover this by reflection or deliberation. Nor is it failure of imagination (*cf.* Williams 1979: 20, quoted on p. 3 above) on his part; the relevant knowledge is just simply not available to him. The reasons exist, tied to objective values (not desire-dependent), but not values that are common. Joining the military is not a good for everyone.

Nor could one say without trivialization that it was a good for everyone *similarly circumstanced*, for the similar circumstance would have to be that one would in fact find the military life to be one's dish of tea. The example can, in this respect, be contrasted with that of the developing music-lover. There we said that listening to Brahms was a good for anyone who had the capacity for *appreciating* Brahms, and that is not the same as to say it is a good for anyone who likes listening to Brahms, or for whom Brahms is just their dish of tea. In the former case we are saying something about Brahms' music, namely that it possesses a certain value which is available to some but not to all; in the latter case we are saying nothing about Brahms' music at all, but only about how certain people are affected by it, and that need not be because they find *the same* value-bearing qualities in it, qualities which are discernible by some but not by all. Similarly, in saying that the military life suits Brown to a T, we are not saying anything about the military life – that it has certain qualities discernible by some, including Brown, but not others – but about Brown, that the military life is just the thing for him. There is nothing analogous here to the appreciation of Brahms. It is simply that the military life is a good for whoever finds it so. And that is why it would be trivial to say it was a good for anyone similarly circumstanced, and foolish to argue for that reason that it was objective in this further sense. It is not trivial, however, to say that Brahms' music is a good for anyone capable of appreciating it – anyone similarly circumstanced in that regard – and not foolish to argue, on those grounds, that it has a different and further kind of objectivity.

Values which depend on personal likes and dislikes, on how things *affect* people exclusively, are thoroughly objective in that they must be discovered and are not subject to the will nor dependent upon desires that 'just come to us', but they are not objective in this further sense. Where the value is *in the object itself*, rather than in its affecting me agreeably, even if that value is not discernible to everyone, it can be said to be objective in the further sense of attaching to the qualities of some object. Aesthetic appreciation is, of course, my paradigm, and it is obvious from what I have said that I am not an aesthetic hedonist. The value of a work of art does not lie in its capacity for 'turning people on', but in certain perceptible properties whose value-bearing character is discernible by persons of a certain innate capacity plus developed taste or discernment. Of course I cannot defend this view here, nor refute aesthetic hedonism, but that does not matter for my present purpose, which is to draw certain distinctions. The point can be made hypothetically. If there is such a thing as aesthetic *appreciation*, as distinct from mere pleasure (and this is not an extreme or uncommon view), then aesthetic value can be said to have this further kind of objectivity.

Now about two kinds of values in particular, namely deontic moral values and the values of long-range self-interest, we should note two things. First, unlike simple likes and dislikes or aesthetic discoveries, they are not typically, and do not require to be, discovered in private encounters, but are commonly supposed to be available to reason, or upon rational reflection. Second, they are the most important kind of values argued by many, including, recently, Rawls and Richards, to be objective, and are those motivating 'considerations' which Nagel argues for in *The Possibility of Altruism*.

We have rejected the notion that the value of ends is subjective in the sense of being derived from desire or its satisfaction, but we have found three degrees of objectivity. First, there is the kind of objective value which a thing possesses for a person when it is liked, enjoyed, or otherwise found inherently valuable. Second, there is the case where an object possesses a value-bearing quality discernible by some but not all agents. And finally, there are the common values of long-range self-interest and moral requirement.[2]

[2]Using the language of Parfit and Nagel (Nagel 1980: 101–2), I would be inclined to say that whereas the values tied to prudence are agent-relative, deontic reasons and values are agent-neutral. But Nagel confines agent-neutral values to what should happen (should be) – the only reason-determining moral values recognized by consequentialists – so excluding the values of actions *per se*. Thus his 'deontological' reasons and values are said to be agent-relative, being reasons *for me* to do something which, as such, are not merely a function of the agent-neutral desirability or undesirability of certain happenings or states of affairs. I cannot enter this controversy here, except to say that reasons must be tied to some good (value), and the good to which deontic reasons are tied is not the good of the agent, but of other persons indifferently. In this sense, at least, these reasons, and values, are agent-neutral.

(Again, note that I am only drawing distinctions here; I am not claiming here that values of the second or third kind actually exist.) The first kind of value provides reasons only for those who happen to like or take an interest in the kind of thing in question. The second kind of value, if it exists, provides reasons for those with certain natural capacities plus training and experience. The third kind of value, if it exists, provides reasons for *everyone*, or at least for all agents who can act on the basis of considered reasons. In cases (1) and (2), the reason may *exist* without the agent's being aware of it, nor can it be recognized or supposed to exist except through the agent's actually encountering the value, or through his supposing it to exist on inductive grounds. No amount of reflection upon his present knowledge and value-beliefs could reveal the value to him, not could it reveal the reason as a reason. In case (3), however, we do expect the reason to be recognizable as such (the value seen) on the basis of rational argument or private rational reflection. Reasons of prudence and morality are supposed to be available, as such (i.e. to be capable of being seen as such) by any rational agent.

I remarked earlier (p. 41) that all reasons, in the sense of grounding reasons, could be construed as external, in that their value-bearing or value-related character (what makes them reasons) in no way depends upon the agent's being *aware* of that character. To the extent that the agent *is* aware of that character, the reasons are also *internal*, i.e. they are capable of motivating that agent, but they are still reasons (of the relevant kind) because of their relation to what the agent can, in principle (given sufficient awareness), recognize as worth having, getting, or doing, and not because of their relation to the agent's independently existing *desires*. The reason *exists* if the value is there to be gained, regardless of whether the agent is aware of it, and its existence is therefore external to the agent's present set of desires. It becomes a reason *for the agent*, i.e. part of his or her intentional world, when he becomes aware of it as a reason (which involves recognition or acknowledgement of the related value). It then becomes internal in that this awareness generates a desire for the valued object, and when that desire is acted upon (succeeds in motivating), the grounding reason *as it is for the agent* and the motivating reason, also so construed, are one and the same. But the grounding reason, as such, is still external in the sense of not being dependent on the agent's desires. This externality (in a sense) of all grounding reasons, can now be seen as a simple reflection of the *objectivity* of all *value*, as distinct from desire and its objects, no matter what kind or degree of objectivity any particular value may have.

Bernard Williams claimed that 'external reasons' (reasons not already tied to the agent's desires) could not exist because it is a part of the 'external reasons theorist's' claim that if an agent deliberated correctly, then he would see the external reason as a reason and would consequently come to have the appropriate motivation (hence the reason would become an internal reason). But that where, as must be the case for it to *be* external, the reason is not tied to any of the agent's desires, which are all that he has to deliberate *upon*, deliberation could have no such result. Thus 'reason cannot give rise to a motivation' and Hume is vindicated.

I argued against this by pointing out that the authentic value for the agent which gives rise to the reason may be unknown to him and hence will not be discoverable by deliberation or reflection (though when it does become known as a value it will generate a desire). Now this response might seem to work for values of the first and second kind, but what of values of the third kind? Both the values of long-range self-interest and of moral requirement or necessity are supposed to be available to reason, hence inherently knowable by anyone independently of any particular experience. So will not any rational agent recognize them upon deliberation, or at least upon rational reflection? And will it not follow from this that they are tied to his already existing desires and so are not genuinely external reasons at all?

There is relatively little problem, I think, with rational prudence. Any rational agent will know, upon reflection, that, so far as his present and future life are concerned, no *time* is *per se* to be given rational preference over any other, since he must live through all of them. (He can do nothing about the past, nor is it of practical concern to him.) He will therefore have some motivation to look after his own future well-being, though whether he will always act upon it is another matter. To act for the sake of one's own overall or long-range self-interest, furthermore, is a paradigmatic example of acting in order to satisfy a reflective desire, or a desire derived from rational reflection, as distinct from an appetite or inclination. Indeed, notoriously, in order to be prudent, one may have to battle one's present appetites and inclinations. Thus I may decide to stop

66

smoking cigarettes because I have come to believe that it increases one's chances of contracting heart disease by a factor of 10. I have a powerful inclination to smoke cigarettes, and my felt aversion to what I perceive as threatening death, pain, or injury, does not operate at a distance in time, i.e. when there is no immediate threat. Nevertheless I want, upon reflection, to live as long and as healthily as possible. Hence I resolve to battle my inclinations, a battle in which I may or may not succeed. The intellectually acknowledged *value* of my own future well-being is the source of the reason which I have to master my inclinations and stop smoking. As far as my present *inclinational desires* are concerned, there is only the desire, at intervals, to light up a cigarette and smoke it. These desires, of course, give me no *reasons* for smoking. If a reason for smoking exists, it is the pleasure that smoking gives, and the relief from the mild distress of unsatisfied craving.

So, where the value (external reason) is the agent's future well-being, that value as a value, hence the related reason as a reason, hence the relevant desire, will be available to him upon reflection (perhaps as a reminder), if it was not a part of his conscious and present motivational set before. Nor need it have been. The reflection can give rise to an entirely new desire. The reason has then, of course, been internalized, and so is no longer 'external' in Williams' restricted sense. But it *was* external. And no 'external reasons theorist' would want to deny that external reasons can *become* internal. On the contrary, the possibility of their becoming internal reasons upon recognition, is a necessary condition of their being reasons at all. Nor, *contra* Nagel, is the agent thinking here of the satisfaction of his future as opposed to his present *desires*. He is thinking rather of what *will be of value or worth* for him in the future, including his having a future at all. If the agent has a *present desire* for his own future well-being, that is *because* reflection reveals it to him as a value worth pursuing. The reason which is a reason because it relates to the agent's future well-being is a reason not because it relates to the agent's present desires (as Williams holds must be the case), nor even because it relates to the agent's *future* desires (as Nagel supposes), but because of its relation to what the agent *intellectually grasps* as a value for him. And this cognition *generates* the relevant desire. So here is the plainest possible example of reason (or cognition) giving rise to a motivation, and Hume is refuted.

Of course the cognition is not *itself* a desire, and hence cannot motivate. (In that respect, Hume was right.) But the desire, which can motivate, is a direct consequence of the cognition. Nagel is wrong in supposing that cognitions, *per se*, can motivate. He is also wrong in seeing reasons of prudence as being tied to future *wants*. Williams is right in denying that cognitions can motivate, but overlooks the possibility that if the cognition is a cognition of something recognized by the agent as a value achievable by action (e.g. his own future well-being), it can generate or *create* a desire. This latter possibility is also overlooked by Nagel. Both Nagel and Williams would as soon ignore value,[3] in the one case denying its existence independently of motivation, in the other case keeping it at arm's length. But value is plainly the key. Nor by now, surely, should there seem anything in the least mysterious about it.

The value of long-range self-interest or one's own future well-being, then, will be recognized, upon reflection, by any rational agent. And failure to take it into account in one's deliberations and to act upon it, when appropriate, *will* count as irrational. We have a case, then, where coming to believe, or perhaps, more commonly, being reminded of the truth of an external reasons statement, can produce a new (or revived) motivation, *and* this cognition, unlike cognition of values of the first and second kind, is the result of mere rational reflection.

We can put this last point in another way by saying that an agent's own future well-being can be shown, by a very simple and easily assessed argument, to *be* a reason for doing something. It is a reason for everyone because it is a common value. And any agent going through this reasoning for himself will see that this is true and that it applies in his own case.

Moral value, like the value of one's own future well-being (long-range self-interest), is also supposed to be available to rational reflection. Moral value is not something we come upon in the course of living, but something supposedly knowable upon reflection by every mature rational agent. Moral reasons are furthermore supposed to be, like reasons of long-range self-interest, reasons for everyone without exception. Reasons of moral obligation or requirement are especially difficult, since they are conceived as *binding*, determining a *necessity* or a *must*, as well as not

[3] In Nagel's case, I refer only to *The Possibility of Altruism* (1970). More recently he has turned directly to the question of value (1977; 1979: 196–213; 1980).

directly relating (as reasons of long-range self-interest do) to the good, benefit, or well-being of the agent. Furthermore all of this derives from the mere analysis of the concept of moral obligation or requirement.[4]

It is the tendency of philosophers nowadays to believe that there can be no reasons of this kind, or if there are, their mere recognition is not adequate to motivate. The motivation must come from elsewhere (externalism). Bernard Williams, Philippa Foot, Gilbert Harman, and Rodger Beehler belong in the first category, John Rawls and David Richards in the second. It is part of my position, however, that one cannot acknowledge something as a reason for doing something (through the recognition of a value), without, as a consequence, having a (reflective) desire to do it, so that if there are deontic moral reasons they must be available to everyone, binding on everyone and, when acknowledged, have some motivational force (create a desire).

Bernard Williams' views have already been sufficiently considered. Deontic moral reasons are, for him, a species of external reason, and consequently do not exist. The views of Foot, Harman, and Beehler are essentially similar to this, in that they all refuse to recognize that something might be a reason for an agent if the end in question is not something the agent is already motivated to pursue. Philippa Foot, like Elizabeth Anscombe before her (Anscombe 1958, Foot 1972a), sees talk about obligation, necessity, and the impossibility of escape from moral requirement, as a mere incantation. The rules or principles of morality *per se* no more provide reasons for acting than do the requirements and prohibitions of etiquette. If one does not happen to *care* about that sort of thing, then one has no reasons. Foot's view could, however, be interpreted as externalist in one sense, for she appears to grant that the content of the so-called 'moral point of view' can be recognized independently of commitment to it. But she is not externalist in another sense since, unlike Richards, she denies that the account of what is to be done from the 'moral point of view' is an account of reasons for action. She is internalist in the most important sense, that one cannot suppose oneself to have a reason without thereby having a possible motive.

Gilbert Harman's insistence upon tying reasons to existing

[4] I shall not rehearse the (basically Kantian) arguments here. But I refer the reader to two earlier papers of mine (1966, 1968).

desires or motivations commits him to the following:

> In saying that it was wrong of Hitler to have ordered the extermination of the Jews we would be saying that Hitler had a reason (every reason in the world) not to do what he did. But what is horrible about someone who did what he did is that he could not have had such a reason. *If he was willing to exterminate a whole people,* there was no reason for him not to do so: this is just what is so terrible about him. [emphasis mine] (1977: 108–9).

We condemn Hitler's *acts* from within our own set of social conventions, but we cannot say that Hitler was *wrong* in what he did (although we can say he was evil) because he did not himself subscribe to those conventions, hence could have had no reason for adhering to them. Another passage expresses the idea more clearly:

> It seems to me highly probable ... that there are no substantive moral demands everyone has a reason to accept. I am inclined to believe that, for any such demand, someone might fail to accept it without being ignorant of relevant facts, without having miscalculated, without having failed to see the consequences of his or her opinions, and without being in any way irrational. You cannot always argue someone into being moral. Much depends on his or her antecedent interests and principles. If his or her principles and interests diverge sufficiently from yours, it may well happen that he or she has no reason to accept your morality (1978: 110).

Again, one has a reason only if one already happens to have the relevant motivation.

Rodger Beehler argues that morality has essentially to do with the good of others, especially the relief of others' suffering, but that moral reasons exist only for those who happen to feel concern or sympathy for that suffering (1978).[5] It is the same point again. Moral reasons, and especially deontic moral reasons, as traditionally conceived, *cannot* exist, because there are no reasons requiring action or abstention that are reasons for everyone. They are reasons for a particular agent only if he or she happens to subscribe to certain social conventions, or to certain principles, or to have certain interests or concerns.

The externalist, on the other hand, holds that there are deontic moral reasons. He even attempts to ground them. (Rawls and Richards offer a contractarian grounding.) But he denies that this mere understanding creates any desire to act in accordance with them. My own claim, as a full-fledged rationalist, must be *both* that

[5] See my review of this book in *Philosophy* 54 (1979), 260–3.

these reasons can be shown to exist *and* that this understanding itself generates a (reflective) desire to act in accordance with them, and further that no matter how weak this desire may be at first, it *can* determine the will.

Bernard Williams wants to have me, and those who wish to argue like me, in the following dilemma. Either one can recognize reasons as existing on the basis of rational reflection alone, in which case one remains quite unmotivated unless or until desire enters the picture from somewhere else (externalism), or if, as seems certain, one cannot recognize something as a reason without having at least some desire (possible motivation) to act accordingly, the reason must be seen as a reason precisely in respect of relating to some already existing want or wants. For otherwise how do we account for the apparently necessary connection between seeing something as a reason and having some desire to act accordingly? Where can the *desire* come from if it is not already there? The third possibility, that beliefs can motivate *on their own* without the aid of desires (though the desires may be there as logical ghosts) – the view of Nagel in *The Possibility of Altruism* – has already been rejected (chapter 2). (For similar views, see Locke 1974, McDowell 1978.)

The key to the solution of this difficulty lies in the recognition that to see something as a reason for doing something is precisely to see (or believe) that the action is worthwhile or valuable in some respect; in the case of reasons tied to the worth of ends, that the end is something worth having, getting, or doing in respect of some desirable character which it has or is supposed to have. So expressed, it is not difficult to see why recognition of a reason as such should *generate* a desire where it does not already exist or reinforce it where it does. Nor is value the *product* of desire, as we have seen, but must always be discovered.

It is true that no reason can be a reason *for* an agent (in his or her understanding) unless it has some motivational force, unless it is possible for the agent to act upon it. In this respect externalism is false. But a reason tied to an authentic value (one that the agent could recognize as such) can exist (i.e. can exist as an 'external' reason) without its being a reason *for an agent* in the sense of being, *qua* reason, an object of his or her awareness (hence an 'internal' reason). It becomes such *when* the value is recognized or acknowledged. The problem arises from leaving value, or at least

71

from leaving *objective* value, whether cognized in experience or simply after rational reflection, out of the picture.

Nor is there, in principle, any difficulty in the notion of cognition (or discovery, or recognition) of value. There is obviously no difficulty in the case of instrumental value. Even the most hard core 'no reason without desire' theorist could accept that we can come to believe (perceive, recognize, discover) that something is a means to a desired end, and *that* is what instrumental value *is*. So here at least is a clear and, one would hope, indisputable case of the cognition of value. Furthermore we can say that this cognition, *together with* the desire for the end *creates* or *generates* a desire for the (supposed) means. The thing is that here the desire for the means, *qua* desire, derives all its motivational force from the already existing desire for the end. There is a sense in which no *new* desire is created, even though the thing now seen as a means was not desired before. The value of the means *is* tied to an already existing desire.

The next step should not be difficult to take. I refer to the discovery, through experience, of the things that give delight, absorb one's interest, are rewarding, or otherwise prove valuable or worthwhile. The discovery of something that one *likes* or *enjoys* or otherwise *finds* worthwhile, gives rise to a desire for that thing where no desire existed before. It is true that some appetites or inclinations are given to us, and true also that their objects, when obtained, normally provide pleasure. But many of the things that most make life worth living are things that we discover for ourselves in the course of living, and these discoveries, which are certainly a species of cognition, give rise to desires. It is these rewards and satisfactions – note *not* desire-satisfactions *per se* (see p. 61 and pp. 45–6 above) – that I have called objective values of the first and second kind – objective because not dependent upon desire. Of course these include the objects of appetites (in respect of their pleasure) which I hope I have succeeded in establishing as objective values too. (Instrumental value is objective in the sense that it is *true or false* that the action is a means to the desired end, though the value only exists because the end is desired. See p. 20 above and pp. 85–6 below.)

A big, but not difficult leap is made with respect to values related to our future well-being or our long-range self-interest, for these are ends that we recognize *upon reflection* to be valuable, and which we desire *as a consequence of this*. These desires are *not* part of the system of *given* desires, the appetites and inclinations, the desires that 'just come to us'. The desire for our own future well-being is not a desire that does or *can* exist independently of reflection, since only by reflection are we able to *conceive* our own future existence as such. Most philosophers of the present day, including the majority of those I have referred to, Foot and Williams on one side, Rawls and Richards on the other, and Nagel somewhere in between, would conceive this as a concern with the satisfaction (or non-frustration) of one's own future *desires*. And that is because they see reasons and/ or values as somehow essentially tied to desires or wants. But it has been sufficiently argued (chapter 3) that desire cannot create or confer value, and that the realization of value consists not in desire-satisfaction, but in coming to possess or preserve or bring into being that which has some kind of worth (or to lessen, avoid, or stave off the evil or undesirable). Concern with one's future well-being is not concern that some or all of one's future desires be satisfied (not frustrated), but that one's future life contain sufficient goods or things worthwhile (rewards, satisfactions in the second sense, other worthwhile ends accomplished), and be free of the worst of evils. (I shall have more to say on the subject of evils in a future chapter.) We are dealing here, then, not with things desired now, nor even things which we will desire in the future, nor with what we regard as goods achievable now by action, but with things that we *now* regard as *future goods*. And it is this present regard (belief), that, by creating reflective desire, makes action on prudential grounds possible.

Nagel (1970) not only sees prudential motivation to be tied to the recognition of the agent's future *wants*, but believes that this recognition can, in its pure cognitive aspect, be sufficient to motivate. But, as we have seen, this runs counter to the Humean truth that cognition cannot *qua cognition* motivate. Richards (1971) sees his Principles of Rational Conduct (PRCs) as those principles which are necessary to produce an optimum economy of want-satisfactions over a lifetime, but which, even when recognized as creating reasons for everyone, will not of themselves motivate. For that one must also *want* to be rational. One may be an irrationalist. One's most powerful want may be to follow the inclinations of the moment, rather than to be rational by following the PRCs and optimizing one's want-satisfactions over one's lifetime. If so, one will be quite unmotivated to follow the PRCs. Richards fails to note the inconsistency here, that *if* my very strongest want is indeed to follow the inclinations of the moment, *and* if what is rational is a function of what I *most want* to do, then in following his inclinations the so-called 'irrationalist' will in fact be being rational, by that criterion. The truth is that one cannot but have some propensity to be motivated by considerations of one's own future well-being, provided one considers it at all. And to fail to do so, or to fail to act on such considerations, where appropriate, is the very paradigm of irrationality. In seeing that his acts are irrational, a rational man must see that he is failing to act for his own good. One *can* be an irrationalist, contrary to what Richards' position implies *if* it is made consistent, in the sense that one can resolve, because one wants it more than anything, to live for the moment with no regard to the future, but an irrationalist *cannot* regard his principle as defensible by reason. It follows that rationally justified conduct cannot consist in acting so as to satisfy one's wants with preference being given to those which are the strongest.

The value of one's future well-being is value of the third kind and is universally shared (common) in addition to being objective. We should be well prepared, then, to consider the possibility that there might be objective *moral* values as well, values which, if they exist, we already know must be universally shared and, in the case of deontic values, reasons that determine a necessity for action or abstention. We know also that deontic moral reasons cannot, unlike the reasons of prudence, be reasons in virtue of their connection with the *agent's* well-being.

One way of expressing this point is to say that the moral 'ought' expresses a categorical imperative, or that one cannot escape moral 'oughts', one's desires or aversions in other respects being simply irrelevant to the matter. That this is built into our conception of deontic morality is undeniable. Therefore in denying that judgments based on moral rules or principles imply categorical imperatives, Philippa Foot is arguing that there is something wrong with our conception of deontic morality, that the *requirement* to obey moral principles is just as, but no more, stringent than the requirement to obey the rules of a club or the rules of etiquette. Yet, she argues, that these latter requirements exist clearly does not provide a reason for everyone, even for club members or members of a particular society or sub-society, to obey them. In addition, for one to have reasons, one must *want* to be a good club member, or one must want to do the done thing or to behave *comme il faut*. We do not say that a reason exists for the club member or the member of some society *regardless* of their desires even if society or the club requires obedience. Similarly one must *want* to be moral in order for moral reasons to exist for oneself. Moral imperatives are as 'hypothetical' as any others (Foot 1972a).

Now this looks, on the face of it, as if the possibility of universally binding moral reasons were being rejected simply on the ground that there can be no reason without a want, present or future, and that there is no necessity compelling one to want to be moral. Some do; others do not. Moral reasons exist for the former but not for the latter. If this was all there was to it, we could simply lump Foot together with Williams, Harman, and Beehler, and dismiss them *en masse* as committing the error, now exposed, of supposing that reasons of all kinds must be tied to wants. And if *no* grounding reasons are tied to wants (as I have claimed), but all are tied to values, it cannot be argued against the possibility of *moral* reasons that there are no universal wants for them to be tied to. Just as we specified the kind of values involved in determining that other reasons for action exist, all we need do is to clarify the nature of the value or values served by adherence to the principles of morality.

Now all of this is true and, indeed, there is no other route to be taken in accounting for the existence of deontic moral reasons. *If* these reasons exist, *then* there must be some universally desirable end which they serve. But there are special problems in connection with deontic moral reasons, or reasons of moral requirement or obligation, which do not exist in the other cases. For to see himself as having a reason for pursuing some end, an agent must see it as something worth *his* seeking or pursuing. Otherwise the reason cannot motivate that agent. And to see something as a reason for doing something *is* to have some motivation to do it (the belief generating the desire). (The externalist alternative has been rejected.) There is no problem about things we enjoy or take delight in, or take an interest in, or find inherently worthwhile in other respects (e.g. the good of those we care about, aesthetic value). This is an unproblematical kind of value. Nor is there any difficulty in seeing how the recognition of such value can create desire and so motivate. And similarly there is no difficulty in understanding the value, for an agent, of rational prudence, nor how such recognition

75

can create desire and so motivate. But what kind of value is it that we would recognize as determining that a reason of moral requirement existed, that would create a desire and so motivate?

What Philippa Foot is pointing out is that to say that an act is morally required is not *in itself* to specify a reason for doing it. And to go on talking about 'rightness' and 'being moral' and 'being required by morality' equally fails to tell us why we should so act:

> The conclusion we should draw is that moral judgments have no better claim to be categorical imperatives than do statements about matters of etiquette. People may indeed follow either morality or etiquette without asking why they should do so, but equally well, they may not. They may ask for reasons and may reasonably refuse to follow either if reasons are not to be found (1972a: 164).

She is quite right in one respect. To say that one morally ought, or that one is morally required, or that one is morally obliged to do (or not to do) a thing is *not* to give a reason for doing it. Rather it is to specify the *kind* of reason or grounding for the action (or abstention) that exists. Whatever the reason or ground of the action is, and *that* must be further specified, it is a deontic moral reason or ground, and *as such* requires action or abstention regardless of what the agent's wants may otherwise be. It requires it of him not as a member of a club or as a well-behaved member of a particular society, but as a rational human agent *per se*.

As I remarked before, Foot implies that we can give an account of what being moral consists in (what the principles of deontic morality are), independently of willing, wishing, or desiring to be moral. For, on her view, one can understand what one must do in order to be moral, while doubting that one has any reason to be moral, and certainly while not *desiring* to be moral. The contrary view is that one cannot see something as morally required without seeing it as providing an overriding and compelling reason for action, and hence without having some motivation to act accordingly. Again, as I remarked before, Foot appears to align herself with the externalists such as Richards, who hold that an account can be given of morality and/or justice, independently of commitment to it. On such a view, anyone is perfectly capable of determining what is just or right, once the formula has been provided, but the motivation must come from elsewhere. (Richards differs from Foot in that he holds that one can recognize one has a *reason* for doing something without as a consequence having any possible motivation for doing it. In this respect, Foot, Williams, Beehler, Harman, and I are on the same side – internalists all.) Yet she does not anywhere give any indication of what she thinks the content of morality might be. Perhaps she is saying *whatever* is held to be morally required – social conventions, principles determined by ideal contractors, principles determined by an ideal observer, or whatever – one can always ask for reasons why one should be bound by these principles or conventions or rules. And I agree it is no good merely affirming that these principles *do* provide reasons. But one is not required to stop at *that*. There is more to it than incantation.

In order to show that there *are* deontic moral reasons, one must show that there is a value or that there are values of a kind such that, when one such is recognized, an agent will necessarily regard everyone, himself included, as having an overriding reason for ensuring that it is secured. One will not, in fact, have succeeded in showing that anything *is* morally *required* without having *ipso facto* shown that reasons of this very special kind exist. And merely affirming that something is morally required is obviously not going to do the job. That something would be prescribed by ideal contractors under certain conditions, or by a dispassionate, disinterested, benevolent observer, or by a person when he askes himself, *qua* rational agent, whether he could universalize the permission of what he proposes to do, does not, *by itself* determine that the act (or abstention) is morally required *in the sense of* providing overriding reasons for all rational agents. The rules of a club require certain behaviour; they do not recommend it. The same is true of the rules of etiquette. These rules are laid out as requirements. But it belongs to our very conception of the principles of deontic morality not merely that they require conduct of a certain kind, but that they provide overriding reasons, valid for everyone, for willing them to be obeyed by everyone (Bond 1968: 168–9). This is perhaps what Foot thinks *does not make sense* (1972a: 164). But we do not simply leave it at that. We attempt to spell out the values, values for everyone, which, if they are recognized, will bring it about that a person *realizes* that he or she is bound by these requirements. That is what a justification of deontic morality would be.

Now it so happens that I do believe that the content of the only

77

possible deontic morality (morality of obligation or rquirement) can be spelled out, indeed can be determined by a formula, independently of recognizing that these principles do bind everyone, myself included, to follow them (Bond 1968). In other words, we can accept this as an account of morality without assenting to its being binding on everyone, requiring of us that we limit our freedom of action in certain ways. For to accept *that* would be to accept that reasons of this kind exist, and would thereby give one the possible motivation for acting as the principles prescribe. So the moral theorist has two tasks, first showing what morality is, and second, showing why everyone is bound to obey it. It is no good producing some account of the nature of morality and then merely *affirming* that everyone is bound to obey. In order to persuade rationally one must succeed in showing that deontic moral values are values indeed, in fact values of the kind that provide reasons of the very special kind that deontic moral reasons necessarily are. And for this it will *not* be necessary to show how these actions relate to wants or valuations or motivational propensities that one already has. In having shown convincingly that moral values are values to be sought by everyone, one will have shown the reasons everyone has for being moral. I think the theory does exist and that the arguments will go through. But here I can only remove objections to the possibility of there being a theory of deontic morality at all. The detailed exposition and argument must wait for another time.

A reason exists for an agent for doing A, when there is some value, in principle recognizable by him as relevant to his own choices, to be gained by doing A. That the value be in principle recognizable by him satisfies the condition that a reason cannot be a reason for an agent unless he can make it his reason for acting. The recognition of the value may come about through an encounter, or through reflection or rational persuasion. We have seen examples of the former in the case of values of the first two kinds, and a clear example of the latter in the case of rational prudence. If there are such things as deontic moral reasons (reasons of moral requirement), their existence must also be available to reflection or rational persuasion. The example of rational prudence shows us that there is no objection *in principle* to the possibility of there being values of this kind.

Does this mean that the person who fails to acknowledge moral reasons, to take account of them in his deliberations, and allow them to determine his choices, is irrational? In the case of things that would prove pleasurable or enjoyable or otherwise inherently worthwhile, we are not compelled to say that an agent is irrational for failing to act on the reasons they provide. He may simply be unaware of them or unaware that these things are goods for him, in which case they will not be available to him for his deliberations. In the case of prudence, where what the agent considers is his own future well-being, we do expect him to take account of such matters in his deliberations, and to allow them, on most occasions, to determine his course of action. A person who does not is said to be unwise, stupid, foolish, or foolhardy, which is a paradigm of one kind of irrationality. Of course there are some acts which in fact have dire consequences for an agent's future well-being, but which he or she could have no reason for believing to have those consequences, and we do not count him or her irrational in the sense of foolish or imprudent for doing those things, but only the person who should have known better and would have, had he had his wits about him. (It is important not to confuse this kind of irrationality with *akrasia*, where an agent knows full well that he has the best possible reasons for not doing what he proposes to do, but he does it anyway because of a powerful inclination or appetite.)

What, then, of reasons of moral requirement? To begin with, when a person has (as we see it) failed to act on such a reason, we do not *say* that he has acted *irrationally*, but that he has acted *immorally*; we do not call him *fool*, but rather a *villain*. There are philosophers who, like Hobbes, would ground morality in rational prudence. For them, moral reasons would be simply a species of prudential reasons, and a villain would be a species of fool. But both I and those whose views I have been criticizing have been considering moral reasons as a species of reason different from and independent of reasons of prudence, as indeed *deontic* moral reasons (reasons of moral requirement) must be. But if moral reasons are available to pure reflective inquiry, is the villain who refuses to acknowledge them irrational in that respect, as the person is who refuses to acknowledge or consider reasons of ordinary rational prudence? We have already noticed that he is not commonly *called* irrational, but that could be simply because we require a nomenclature that makes clear and does not blur the distinction between fools and villains,

79

between persons who are unwise and persons who are wicked and immoral. The reason, in other words, why we do not *say* that wicked and immoral people are irrational in respect of their wickedness and immorality, could be in order to avoid being misconstrued as saying that they are unwise and imprudent. However, the reasons *are* (by hypothesis) of quite different types. So that if *we* were to say that wicked and immoral men and women are irrational, we would not *have* to be construed as saying that they are unwise or imprudent, as assimilating wickedness to foolishness, morality to prudence. In other words it might be *true* that immorality was a species of irrationality, though, for the reasons given, this was never *said*. Failure to consider or to take into account or, if taken into account, to act upon *one* kind of reason that should be apparent and *is* available to ordinary reflection might be imprudence or foolishness; failure to consider or take into account or, if taken into account, to act upon *another* kind of reason that should be apparent and is available to ordinary reflection might be immorality or wickedness.

But there is something here that does not quite ring true, and that is because, although imprudence or foolishness may be seen, typically, to consist in a failure of (practical) reasoning, the fault of the worst kind of immorality or wickedness is thought to lie in the action itself. The foolish or imprudent act is characteristically a consequence of a failure to reason as any normal, mature person might be expected to reason or, if not that, a failure to act, through weakness of will, as practical reason directs. (I am assuming that the genuine irrationalist (see pp. 73–4 above) is extremely rare.) Wicked and immoral acts, however, need not be, and, in the worst cases, are not, the consequence of a failure to reason or to reason adequately, nor is wickedness a kind of weakness of will (though *akrasia* may result in knowing or conscious immorality). And it is not just that the devious, dishonest, unprincipled scoundrel is shown, if he is successful, to be *very good* at reasoning with respect to his own self-interest. His failure is not a failure to note that his proposed acts are immoral and to take this into account in making his decisions. The wickedest villains scoff at the very idea of (what they regard as conventional) morality, and knowingly take advantage of others' (as they see it) foolish commitment to it.

I said, only a few pages back, that a moral theory might convincingly show that there are moral values which should be sought by everyone, that there are deontic moral reasons which are reasons for everyone. And, of course, anyone who was persuaded of the truth of such a theory would, *ipso facto*, acknowledge these reasons to be reasons, and hence would have a possible motivation for acting in accordance with them. But this was partly a confession of faith, for I do not believe that, in spite of many partly successful efforts, the completely adequate theory has yet been produced. *A fortiori* we cannot expect people to be motivated to righteousness on the basis of a correct theoretical understanding of the nature and grounds of morality! Yet we do, not only in law, but in ordinary daily contexts, expect people to, as we put it, 'know the difference between right and wrong.' We hold people responsible for their moral failings simply in virtue of their being normal and normally endowed, mature human beings. Or if we do speak of reduced responsibility, that is understood to exist because of a *failure of rationality*. Small children, madmen, idiots, the senile, are among those supposed not to have full moral responsibility for their acts. And this is not thought to be a matter of correct upbringing or knowledge of the conventions of one's society; it is something thought to be available to all rational persons. There are stock phrases (many of which philosophers have unsuccessfully sought to elevate into theories) which are used in order to draw a child or another person's attention to the moral aspect of a situation: 'How would you like it if somebody did that to you?' 'What would it be like if everybody did it?' 'We couldn't have people allowed to go around doing that sort of thing whenever they felt like it.' 'What if the shoe were on the other foot?' 'Other people have feelings too.' And so on, and so forth. And there are strong grounds for saying (no matter what philosophers say) that *everyone knows* that being immoral consists in placing oneself in a special position of superiority or advantage *vis-à-vis* others, a position for which one can offer no publicly acceptable justification, or of acting in ways that one could not rationally will others to do at their pleasure (that one *must* rationally will others *not* to do at their pleasure). The assumption is that those who are guilty and can be held responsible for wrong or immoral acts know that their acts are wrong or immoral. But this lands us right back in our difficulty, because what the knowing and willing immoralist does is precisely *not* to treat moral considerations as reasons for him. Yet there are others who do recognize moral reasons as reasons and are motivated accordingly or feel guilty if they do not.

We must conclude from all this that the fundamental *content* of deontic morality is or can be known or roughly known to all normal and normally endowed mature persons, but that not all normal and normally endowed mature persons are compelled to recognize that deontic moral considerations have a claim on them. They are not compelled to recognize deontic moral values, to recognize that deontic moral reasons exist objectively and hence are reasons for all persons, themselves included. Yet either such reasons exist objectively or they do not. There are many, including many non-believers in any divine sanction or authority, or social or parental authority either, for that matter, who do suppose such reasons to exist. And if they are right, as I believe they are, then they have seen something which others have failed to see. There must be some *failure of cognition* on the part of the willing immoralist.

Alan Gewirth (1978) argues that this is a failure of consistency in reasoning, a failure to grant rights to others on the same grounds that I claim them for myself, but I do not think that this is so.[6] The egoist and the immoralist are guilty of no contradiction when they deny that moral considerations are reasons for them (that they are really reasons at all). Rather they have failed to recognize that whatever value or worth their own well-being has, the well-being of others has exactly the same value or worth. It is the failure to stand back from oneself and see oneself simply as one person among many, the incapacity or unwillingness to take an objective view. In this respect Nagel (1970: 99–115) is very close to the truth. Of course one does not cease to be oneself, nor to have one's own desires, interests, pleasures, and projects which, for obvious reasons, have a special place in one's own life that the desires, interests, of others do not. Everyone does not, as Nagel seems to imply,[7] have to adopt the reasons tied to everyone else's good equally with those tied to his own. To suppose one has to adopt *that*

[6]See my symposium with Gewirth on this book (Bond & Gewirth 1980). Unfortunately there is a line of type missing on p. 53. The penultimate sentence should read: 'Whatever reality and importance your well-being has, the well-being of every similar subject-agent has just the same kind of reality and importance.'
[7]The reference here is to *The Possibility of Altruism* (1970). Nagel's views, as the Oxford Tanner Lectures (1980) reveal, have since changed considerably. Everyone still has an obligation to pursue the agent-neutral values of the consequentialist, but this obligation is now seen as limited by (1) reasons relating to the pursuit of an agent's *own* ends (reasons of autonomy), now no longer said to be agent-neutral, and

kind of objectivity becomes mere foolishness. And people should, in any case, be free to pursue their own ends. But one must be prepared to *accommodate* one's own well-being to the well-being of others by not adopting modes of conduct that one could not be willing to have others adopt at their pleasure.

So what are we to say about the agent who fails to take moral reasons into account in his deliberations? Is he irrational? Certainly not in the sense that he is imprudent or in the sense that he is inconsistent. And failure to be able to see oneself as just one among many is a common failure, even among those who have seen the point and do desire to be moral. Further there are no doubt many egoists and immoralists for whom all attempts at rational persuasion must fail. But if deontic moral reasons do exist, this nevertheless *is* a failure of cognition. Of course if, because of this failure, these reasons are simply not available to the wicked and immoral man or woman for his or her deliberations, we cannot say he or she is irrational, any more than we can say that a man or a woman is irrational for failing to act to attain some good for himself or herself of which he or she is unaware. In this respect immorality is different from imprudence – for little effort is required to recognize the value and importance of one's own well-being over time.

(2) deontological reasons (reasons why *I* should not maltreat others, hence agent-relative and not consequentialist). My suspicion is that the agent-neutral reasons of utilitarianism will eventually disappear altogether from Nagel's account of personal morality and be confined to the political realm. At least this is what I think ought to happen.

5

Objective value – II

I argued in the last chapter that, in a sense, all values were objective, in the same sense, namely, that all values were 'external', i.e. their existence was independent of desire and will. But I have so far said little or nothing on the subject of whether values are objective in the sense of being 'part of the fabric of reality', of how they can be *known*, about whether value judgments can be said to be *true* (as objectivity seems to imply) or whether there are assertibility conditions that fall short of being truth conditions. I have said little, in other words, on the ontological status of values, or on the subject of what might be called 'axiological epistemology'.

This has been quite intentional on my part, for I wished to show by easy stages how and in what respects different sorts of value, worth, goodness, desirability (these are rough synonyms) – in general that which is worth having, getting, or doing – had to be construed as objective. Note that my position is a strong one. I am not claiming that some value is objective (e.g. moral value, prudential value) but that all value is *necessarily* objective, in the sense that it is never a function of desire (or the will); nothing is ever valuable or desirable *in virtue of* being desired. (I am, of course, speaking in the present context of the worth or value of actions or their ends, values as they relate to practical rationality and judgment. There are many things which I may acknowledge, no doubt often correctly, to possess value, or to have valuable characteristics, that do not provide me with reasons for action, that do not bear on my practical judgment. But I would suppose that, *a fortiori*, these values are not the product of desire.)

I have hoped, by presenting my argument for objectivity in the way I have, to disarm the so-called 'argument from queerness', summarized as follows by Mackie:

This has two parts, one metaphysical, the other epistemological. If there were objective values, then they would be entities or qualities or relations of a very strange sort, utterly different from anything else in the universe.

84

Correspondingly, if we were aware of them, it would have to be by some special faculty of moral perception or intuition, utterly different from our ordinary ways of knowing everything else (1977: 38).

Mackie is, of course, talking about moral values in particular, but the argument from queerness is usually thought to apply to the claim that *any* sort of value is objective. What sort of entity, property, or relation could this funny kind of thing, a value, be? How could we perceive or otherwise know such objects? And if we approach the question from this general, abstract, ontological and epistemological point of view, we are going to begin thinking that the whole thing has a queer ring. There are many who fear that accepting the objectivity of value would, of necessity, lead them into some kind of disreputable intuitionism, even Platonism; there they are, the values, somehow existing *out there*, part of the fabric of the universe. Could anything be more absurd than that? Is it not apparent that value is nothing but a reflection of desires, emotions, 'pro-attitudes', and other subjective states? Is not this the most plausible view? Does it not make for a neater ontology? Does it not forestall altogether problems about how there could be such a (queer) thing as knowledge of values? Is it not absurd to suppose that value might exist in the universe without persons (or other animals) and their appetites, inclinations, and purposes? And if so, are they not dependent on these things? Yet the doctrine of the objectivity of value seems to imply that values have an independent existence, even if there were no persons, even if there were no conscious appetitive agents in the world. And surely that simply cannot be swallowed. Values exist only for those who have desires, aims, 'concerns', projects, purposes, and they are a function of these. That is the only reasonable view.

But compare these abstract ontological and epistemological worries, seeming to lead inevitably to the subjectivity or relativity of value, to what has already been argued here on the subject in a way that, up to a point at least, is commonsensical and not at all mysterious. (1) One can perceive something as a means to a desired end. This is to perceive it as having instrumental value. This is the first baby step and it ought to wipe out at once the fear that talk about cognition of value must lead to intuitionism or Platonism. For there is no question that this is a species of value, and there is equally no question that it is objective. Either it is or it is not an (efficient) means to a desired end, and that is a simple matter of fact. No ontological problems; no epistemological problems. Its being a value simply *consists* in its being the means to a desired end. What does it mean for the value to *exist*? It is a necessary and sufficient condition of the value's existing (the act's having instrumental value) that it *is* an (efficient) means to a desired end. This is *all* it means, or could mean, to say that value exists. There is no ontological problem. We do not have to assign it to a special realm of being! How can this value be known? One comes to know the act's *utility* (and that is the kind of value in question here) simply in recognizing that it is an (efficient) means to the desired end. Do we need a special faculty of intuition? No. There is no epistemological problem. It is a sufficient condition of the existence of the value of utility *in general* that there are things which are (efficient) means to desired ends. About utility, a quite genuine and quite genuinely objective value, there is no mystery whatever.

But, it will be objected, there is an obvious sense in which the value of utility is dependent upon desire. For a thing possesses this value precisely in virtue of being the means to a desired end. Of course that is true, and if the end were not desired, the means would not possess the value of utility (see p. 20 above). But still – and this is the important point – the means does not possess the value of utility in virtue of *its* being desired; the value of the means lies in its *efficiency* in accomplishing the desired end. *And that is an objective matter that is not dependent on desire.* Note there is no need to suppose that the mere desire for an end imparts value to it, and that the means has value as a consequence of that, something I argued against at length in chapter 3. A thing possesses the value of utility simply in virtue of being an efficient means to a desired end, leaving the question of the value of that end entirely aside. (It may, in fact, have none at all.) Thus my general position remains intact: *nothing possesses value simply in virtue of being desired.*[1]

But, in that its existence in no way depends on the value of, as distinct from the desire for the end, instrumental value (utility) is unique, and it is false extrapolation from this more than anything else that has led people to suppose that one cannot ask questions about the value of ends, that one must simply take the end as given.

[1] For the so-called 'primary' or 'basic' goods (Rawls 1971, Gewirth 1978), certain instrumental goods the absence of which are universal evils, see chapter 7, especially pp. 123–4, 129–31, 133.

But let us consider desirable ends. What of the things that I discover, through experience, that I like, that please me, that give me satisfaction, that relax me, that make me feel good. Here is a cluster of inherent values – i.e. values possessed by ends – and every one of them is as objective as can be, for while every one of them gives rise to desire, none of them is the product or consequence of desire. They are things I must find out about. The values (value characters) in question here are the pleasant, the agreeable, the satisfying, the relaxing, the spirit-raising or enlivening – undeniable, all of them, and undeniably not identical with the satisfaction of some pre-existing desire, which satisfaction, if such a desire exists at all, does not guarantee their production in the least. We may call them, for the sake of convenience, *hedonic* values, and we can include among them the pleasure that is normally consequent upon the satisfaction of appetites, and sometimes consequent upon the satisfaction of reflective desires. (That the value of such pleasure is not simply a function of the desire in question is a point I have already argued in chapters 3 and 4.)

Well, what of the ontological problem? What is it for such values to exist? It is a sufficient condition of (e.g.) golf's being enjoyable or relaxing, hence valuable, for me, that when I play the game I normally relax and/or enjoy myself. It is a sufficient condition of the existence of the pleasant or the satisfying *in general*, that some things are found by some persons to be pleasant or to give satisfaction. Again no question of any resort to intuitionism or Platonism, or of having to assign these objective values to some special Meinongian realm. Nor is there an epistemological problem. I am unlikely to be mistaken (although I can deceive myself) in supposing that I am enjoying or that I do (normally) enjoy or take pleasure in some activity or experience. In any case I do not need intuition nor any faculty that will give me access to mysterious Platonic realms! There is no more of an epistemological problem about values of this kind than there was about utility.

Again, if we ask abstractly how values can be objective, what these strange things could be, and how we could have access to them, it all seems very queer. But when we begin to examine some actual values the queerness vanishes altogether and we are left in the realm of ordinary common sense. The trouble is that in our abstract talk about values we forget what values are!

Admittedly there is a little more difficulty in the case of valuable characteristics which are supposed to inhere in objects as objects of experience, of which aesthetic values are the paradigm. It is especially difficult because the value-bearing characters are supposed to lie on the 'aesthetic surface', there to be discovered on acquaintance but not precisely described. But in so far as aesthetic values can be named, as they are in the language of criticism, there is, I think, no special ontological or epistemological problem. Consider, for example, the grace of the gazelle, the expressiveness of Cortot playing Chopin, the majesty of the opening of Bruckner's 9th Symphony, the grandeur of the cathedral of Chartres. These things are there to be observed, and those who have experienced them know what is being referred to here. They are there to be found, of course, in the object as an object of experience, and hence are not objective in the sense that the molecular structure of this table or the gravitational power of the sun might be held to be objective. But then it is not *that* kind of objectivity that we are talking about. By that criterion, no directly perceived quality, such as colour, is objective. But that an object is of a certain colour is an objective and determinable matter of fact. Although, it is objective only for human beings or other beings similarly constituted. And I do not wish to make any greater claim for value. Clearly it would be absurd to do so in the case of pleasure, relaxation, and feeling good, or for that matter, utility. Yet all are thoroughly objective and they do not depend upon desire. Utility excepted, they are valuable in that they constitute rewards. They are inherently desirable kinds of lived experience. (I shall return in chapters 6 and 8 to the question of the relation between the existence of value and subjective states.)

There seems to be no particular difficulty about values tied to long-range self-interest or one's own future well-being, since this kind of value is dependent upon what is already acknowledged to be good or valuable for an agent at any *particular* time. It is the value, simply, of providing for, or ensuring goods for the future and preventing preventable evils. The recognition of it as a value comes with the recognition that every moment of one's present and future life is as important as any other; that the time at which one is or will be engaging in activity or having an experience is not, in and of itself, relevant to its value. (It must be remembered that our concern throughout is with value achievable by action, the only kind of value with which practical rationality can be concerned. Of course value – both good and evil – may lie in the past, but it was either there, realized, or it was not; nothing can now be done about it.)

To say, then, that the value of one's future well-being or long-range self-interest, hence the virtue of prudence, *exists*, is to say no more than this. Again we do not need to search for some appropriate realm of being. Nor is there an epistemological problem. To recognize the value of one's future well-being or long-range self-interest is nothing more than to recognize the equal importance, from one's own practical point of view, of every lived moment from the present to the end of one's conscious life, and hence that everything is not to be rashly sacrificed to the joys of the present moment. There is such a virtue as prudence, and we can recognize it and its ends as values. Nor is there anything queer, mysterious, or unpalatably intuitionist, Meinongian, or Platonic about this.

One thing has been omitted, however, from this account, and that is the value of life itself. For an important part of prudence is taking care to ensure that one is not killed, or does not die of any cause, acting so as to ensure that one lives a long as well as a healthy and prosperous life. An important part of what makes life worth living is the good that it contains, and the absence of at least the worst of evils (of the kind that are to be lived through or endured). An important part of what makes life *seem* worth living, and hence of what makes one reflectively desire to go on living, is the prospect of these things or, in other words, the prospect of joy in one's activities, projects, and experiences, and only of such sorrows as are bearable. So the value of life is itself partly dependent upon those same values (joys, rewards) to which the value (well-being over time) which makes prudence a virtue itself is tied. So, in this respect at least, there is no ontological or epistemological queerness in acknowledging that the value of life exists objectively.

There seems to be as well, however, a value in simply being alive, conscious, and active; and similarly, extinction (ceasing to be) is thought to be an inherent evil and not an evil only because it puts an end to all our joys. But here too one can acknowledge the inherent value of conscious and active life (being) without ontological or epistemological indigestibility. (This subject is taken up again on pp. 127–9 below.) And let us note once more, even if only as an incantation to purge us of the fallacy, that this has nothing to do, *per se*, with desires or their satisfaction. Desires do not create value and their satisfaction does not realize it.

Is moral value, then, the stumbling block? We have seen that there is no ontological or epistemological problem about the objective existence of many kinds of value, so that one cannot deny the existence of moral value(s) on the grounds that, because of the queerness, no value can exist objectively. And we have done down the bogey who, on other grounds, now exposed as fallacious, would repeat to us that value is created by desire and realized in its satisfaction or, on similar grounds, that there is no value but only the satisfaction of desire. So where is the problem about moral value?

The problem is, bluntly, that whereas all the values so far examined bear on the good, the well-being, the happiness of the agent (for whom the value is one achievable by a certain action at the time, so providing him with a reason for that action), many moral values, and especially deontic moral values, are not values in virtue of how they benefit, profit, delight, or please the *agent*, but in respect of some other grounds altogether such as, e.g. preventing harm to others. The problem, as Philippa Foot saw it, was how such a reason can be a reason if it is not tied to the agent's wants. This view of the problem has now been found wanting. But there is a genuine question of how a reason can be a reason for an agent if it is not somehow tied to his or her own *good* – his or her own interest, profit, welfare, pleasure, or whatever.

It has already been stated that for a reason to be genuine for an agent, it must be tied to a value that he himself could, given the right conditions, recognize as such, and consequently be motivated to pursue. It is not difficult at all to see how a want can be generated by the recognition that something will benefit or profit or please one in some way. It is more difficult to see how a want can be generated *of necessity* by abstract considerations of the good of others, or the good of society, or justice, or the reconciliation of conflicting interests, or things of a similar kind.

Rawls thinks you can, by rational persuasion, show a thing to be required by justice without as a consequence giving anyone any motive for acting accordingly. To do that you must persuade a person that justice is, to use his expression, *congruent* with his own good (his own good in turn interpreted in terms of desire-satisfactions). Richards thinks that the principles of morality determine reasons for all persons which they can recognize as such, but that the motivation to act in accordance with them must come from elsewhere. This contradicts the principle accepted by all internalists, myself included, that to see oneself as having a reason for doing something is *ipso facto* to have *some* motivational direction towards it. (I hold it on the grounds that to think one has a reason is to think that there is something of worth to be gained by one's action, that the act is, in some respect, worth doing. Williams, Harman, and Beehler hold it because for them one has a reason only if one has a want.)

Nagel's view, that such considerations (justice, preventing harm to others, etc.), when properly grasped as reasons, can motivate just by themselves and without any desire, has already been rejected. And it is ironic in this connection that Nagel insists on maintaining the connection between reasons and *wants*, so that seeing something as an (objective) reason is to see an action as satisfying some want or other (present or future, mine or another's), when the sole ground for attaching grounding reasons to wants in the first place was the mistaken identification of them with motivating reasons, which really *are* tied to the actually existing wants of the agent! In other words, Nagel is arguing, in effect, that justifying or grounding reasons (though he would not, or would not have in *The Possibility of Altruism*, acknowledged their existence), must be tied to wants (though not necessarily to present wants), while motivating reasons require no wants in order to motivate. And this is the very reverse of the truth! (Motivating reasons require desires or wants; grounding or justifying reasons do not, but rather require *values*, values that are, in principle, recognizable by the agent.)

The challenge here is to produce a moral theory that would give (a) an account of the content of deontic morality, and (b) an account of the reasons we have for being moral rather than choosing to be egoists or immoralists. We all have a very good idea of the content of deontic morality – it has to do with the restrictions which (it is supposed) we must place on our freedom to pursue our own ends, in the interests of others. Any persuasive justification of morality, i.e. any persuasive account of how it is that we all have reasons for regarding moral considerations as reasons for everyone, hence for ourselves, would, *eo ipso*, have demonstrated the value or worth of acting morally.

The important thing to note here is that recognizing this underlying value and the values that derive from it, which are the moral values, is not incipient Platonism. There is no more *ontological* difficulty with this kind of value than there is with any of the other kinds of value that have been mentioned. For saying that such values exist is no more than saying that other persons, conceived as rational, sentient subject–agents like oneself, are real, that they matter, that they count, in just the same way as one matters or counts oneself. Nor need we call upon any special faculty of intuition to grasp this kind of value. There is no difficulty whatever in grasping it; it is, in fact, a point that can be made plain to a child. Even if one does not care about others, one must acknowledge their existence for themselves and the importance *for them* of the good and evil that befall them, which is exactly the same importance that the good and evil that befall you have *for you*. And this recognition can motivate one to be moral regardless of whether one happens to care in one's heart for the people who are or who may be affected by one's actions.

I have said that there only appears to be an ontological and epistemological difficulty about objective values – that the argument from queerness only gains a foothold – if we consider the question *in abstracto*, forgetting what value *is*. There is another question concerning how it can be that if desirability (goodness, value, worth) is objective and statements to the effect that a certain aim or end is good or worthwhile or valuable or desirable are capable of being true or false, hence capable of being known (as well as truly or falsely believed), how such knowledge or belief can be *internally* tied to desire and the possibility of motivation. For, after all, questions of value are by their very nature practical (that is if the value is one achievable by action), and how can this be so if the possession of value is just another objective state of affairs, to be cognized in the ordinary way? Or, to put it another way, how can a state of affairs, existing objectively to be perceived, or discovered, or understood upon reflection or rational persuasion, *of its very nature*, as apprehended, have a role in determining what one does? How can a question of what is objectively the case have a necessary bearing, not only on the question of what one should do, but on one's actual motivation? And the answer appears to be, when the question is considered *in abstracto*, that it cannot. I wish to argue that this is simply another instance of forgetting what a value is, and that reminding ourselves is the first and most important step towards solving the problem.

Readers will notice a certain resemblance between this problem and the much discussed question of the relationship between fact and value. But the differences are extremely important. Those who hold that there is an unbridgeable gap between fact and value (non-cognitivists) are already treating value as necessarily subjective because of its supposed internal tie to desire and motivation. (The truth is that one cannot value something as an end of action, i.e. *regard* it as valuable, without having some motivational propensity towards that thing.) And no fact (something that is merely true or false), they say, can have this sort of tie or can induce this motivational propensity as a necessary consequence of being believed. Their belief is that value is a *product* of desire, or that to desire a thing, to value it, and for it to *be* valuable for the valuer–desirer, are one and the same thing. They have coined the word 'pro-attitude' to cover all these things. Values involve pro-attitudes, they say, and pro-attitudes neither are, nor are inferable from, facts. Naturalists, on the other hand, want to argue that values *are* inferable from facts, that they are, therefore, a species of fact, some-times a fact connected with what people want (Foot 1958), sometimes an institutional fact (Searle 1964). In the former case, the necessary tie to motivation is maintained; in the latter case, it is severed.

However, I have taken value out of the realm of the subjective (as being a product of, or one and the same with, or the shadow of, desire or, for that matter, will (cf. Sartre 1946)), and have argued that, even in the case of hedonic value, an object's having value is no product of desire or the will, but needs to be discovered. In the problem as I have just now presented it, value has ceased to be on the subjective side of the gap. It has moved over to the objective side, and left on the subjective side now are 'ought'-judgments and desires (motivational propensities). One thing we can do at once is to move the 'ought' or 'should' judgments over to the side of value, noting the internal (or conceptual or analytic) tie between values achievable by action and 'ought' or 'should'. But if values remain objective, one would now query how one could get from such a 'should' (one internally tied to an objective value) to a desire and hence a motive.

Let us return for a moment to the discovery of hedonic value. Here to discover the value of something is to discover that one *likes* it. One's liking of the thing was not (and could not have been) created by one's will, nor could it have been created by one's desire for it. Of course experiencing it will *create* a desire for it and there, really, is the solution to our problem at least for this kind of case. I did not make the hedonic value by my will or my desire; I discovered it only by experience or experiment. But I have experienced the joy of the thing and I recognize it as a good for me; I acquire both an inclination towards it (as a psychological effect of the experience) *and also* a reflective desire coming about as a consequence of my now seeing it (consciously, reflectively) as a good. The inclination may motivate me without deliberation; my conscious and reflective recognition of it as a good may play a role in my deliberation and possibly determine its outcome on some occasions, as it may the subsequent action. And that is how the pattern works. What kind of a value has it for me? I delight in it for its own sake; it gives me joy or pleasure (an easily understood kind of value). Because it has delighted me, I now know the character (quality, aspect) that delights me (that I find delightful). In recognizing that this value exists for me, I recognize *that I have a reason* for seeking the thing out on appropriate occasions in the future, namely the reason that it will (or is likely to) delight me. This reason will be able to *count* in my deliberations because the recognition of the value has given rise to a reflective desire for the kind of thing in question.

And the same pattern will apply for other kinds of value, given that they are values for the agent, achievable by his or her action, and which he or she can, given the right conditions, recognize as such. What kind of value has x for me? It gives me financial protection in unforeseeable emergencies, and it is worth the present cost. I see that it is in my long-range self-interest. Seeing it as valuable in this respect, I conceive a reflective desire for it. This reason (as I see it) determines the outcome of my deliberation, and I act on this desire and in order to achieve this end. In the deontic moral case, everything will depend, of course, on being able to make out that deontic moral reasons are reasons for everyone (that deontic moral values exist). But if one accepts a deontic moral reason as a reason in respect of being tied to a special kind of value, which one accepts as worth one's pursuing, the pattern is the same. In recognizing the value achievable (including evils preventable, avoidable, or alleviable) by one's action (or abstention), one recognizes that one has a reason and, at the same time, conceives a reflective desire for the end in question, a desire which may motivate.

What makes the hedonic case different from the others is that, in addition to the reflective desire which follows upon the discovery of the value and its recognition as a value (a good), there is the purely psychological effect of one's henceforth being inclined to seek the kind of thing in question when it is thought to be available. But the existence of this inclination has nothing to do with practical rationality or even with rational motivation. As with all appetites and inclinations, one can act to satisfy that inclination without deliberation and without even considering whether one does or does not have a reason for doing what one does. This would be an act done for reasons, namely to satisfy an inclination, but not a rationally motivated act, i.e. one done as a consequence of noting that one has a reason (noting that there is something of worth to be gained by the action) and acting for the reason that one then supposes one has.

Thus the supposed epistemological difficulty in moving from something objective which is discovered or recognized, through a series of necessary or internal steps to something which has, of its own nature, an effect on one's motivational state, is overcome as soon as we cease to consider the problem as an epistemological problem in general terms and consider what an objective value is. An objective value is not, of course, value-neutral! But that does not mean that it is a product of desire. Nor does it mean that it is desire-dependent in any way. However the recognition of the value as a value, hence the recognition that one has a reason, will, given what such a recognition is, have, of necessity, an effect on one's motivational state for it will *create a desire*, a reflective desire as distinct from an inclination, that *can* motivate.

This simple resolution of the problem also provides the key to the solution of the above-mentioned (p. 93) controversy between non-cognitivists, who insist that value-judgments contain an irrevocably subjective element of 'attitude' or 'commitment of the will', and naturalists who insist that value, including moral value, is to be found in the world of facts. In fact, both positions are wrong, though both contain important truths: non-cognitivism the truth that there is a necessary connection between value-beliefs and motivation; naturalism the truth that not just anything at all can count as a value. Non-cognitivism is false because values can be cognized and value judgments are capable of being true or false; naturalism is false because, in a peculiar way, it leaves value, i.e. *being of worth*, out of the picture altogether. Of course recognition of something as being of worth (and attainable by action) *creates* a motivation, and that is how the important truths on both sides of the controversy are retained while what is false is expunged.

But not all that it is necessary to say about the nature of objective value has been said. To state a most obvious point, even if I have succeeded in showing that value is not desire-dependent, it is plainly, on the account I have been giving, *subject*-dependent. I should like to say at once that I acknowledge this to be both true and important, and also that this does not count in any way against its objectivity in the sense in which I am claiming that values are (necessarily) objective. In fact much of the initial plausibility of the argument from queerness comes from the supposition that if something is to be objective it cannot be subject-dependent, yet not even the most rampant empiricist or phenomenalist has wished to deny some form of objectivity. No one has ever seriously advocated solipsism!

An empiricist might be construed as a person who wishes to claim that everything was subject-dependent, at least in the sense of experience-dependent. (Only Hume, and Russell, in his neutral-monist stage, saw the world in terms of independently subsisting bits of experience unattached to any priorly existing subject.) But one does not need to be an empiricist to acknowledge that much of the world that we commonly inhabit, and which is the subject of our discourse and our thought, is the world as it is for human beings and, in some cases, the world as it is for human beings of a particular time and place. Neither of these constitute objectivity in the classical Galilean sense of things as they are in themselves quite independently of how observers are affected by them. Yet neither of them is purely subjective in the sense of adverting only to the content of some private individual's intentional realm – the world as it is for Christopher Brown.

The question is where, exactly, am I claiming that value is located? I have included, for example, personal likes and dislikes in the realm of objective value, whereas others would regard these as subjective. The values of prudence and deontic morality, however, seem to belong straightforwardly to the world as it is for human beings. But, in that case, is there no place in my scheme for values that belong to the world as it is for persons of a particular place and time, i.e. of a particular culture? This must all be sorted out.

Different individuals take delight in, take pleasure in, or otherwise find inherently valuable or worthwhile, different things – different activities, sensations, experiences, and states of affairs. This is an obvious truth and, furthermore, not something to regret in the least. More than this, different individuals are only capable of delighting in certain things and not in others. It is not simply a case of some individuals not having been exposed to the things in which others find delight, or having been given insufficient time to acquire a taste for them. In respect of what may or may not delight them, and what they may or may not find unpleasant, different individuals have different natures. One man's meat is another man's poison. In some cases, as in the case of aesthetic value, we can say that the value-bearing characters exist objectively – out there on the aesthetic surfaces – to be appreciated by those who have the capacity, but even here there is plenty of room for personal taste. I can enjoy music of a certain genre (e.g. Viennese operetta or Hollywood film music) which I *know* is kitsch, and I can fail to enjoy looking at paintings by someone (e.g. Renoir, Rouault) the worth of whose work I nevertheless am able to acknowledge – not on inductive grounds, but at first hand. So it is personal taste or preference that I am talking about now, and I have claimed some sort of objectivity for it.

The grounds on which I have claimed such objectivity are that a person cannot know (though he may have solid inductive grounds for believing) that something will be rewarding for him in this way until he has *tried* it, and perhaps not even until it has been tried several times. Such value certainly cannot be created by desiring or by wishing or by willing. (I may wish I enjoyed great art, but my wish is not self-fulfilling!) It is objective in the sense that it must be *found out*. It cannot be the case that something will please me because I have an appetite, an inclination, or, for that matter, a reflective desire for it (though I may desire it because it pleases me). Nor can I make it the case that something will please me. Either it will or it will not, and that it will or will not is affected neither by my desire nor by my will. Its pleasing me is therefore, in a sense, *out there* for me, for I must *discover* those delights. Nor (unlike the aesthetic case)

97

need the things found to be enjoyable be construed as phenomenally or intentionally objective. This is most obvious in the case of pleasurable *sensations*, where the thing enjoyed is clearly internal and experienced as such.

Yet 'pleasant', 'delightful', 'fun', 'agreeable', 'enjoyable', and so forth, are all desirability characteristics. Delighting in something for its own sake is a kind of universal and common value. Though the things that are found to be delightful (or unpleasant) are different for different people, doing what you like doing (or having the experiences you like having) is a value or a good for everyone. In other words, hedonic value is a common good. And let there be no confusion about this. Hedonic good *lies in* the delightful or agreeable character of the object, activity, sensation, or other experience, and this has nothing to do with its being wanted. There are some, like Rawls, who would claim that the only common (or general, or basic) goods are those things that are *desired by everybody*, and others who say that some things are common goods because they are *valued* by everybody. It would be absurd to claim that either of these things was true of pleasure. It is inherently good, or good in virtue of its very nature; it is furthermore a kind of value that can be immediately felt, acknowledged, recognized. It is certainly true that most people desire pleasure, and that most people value it as well, but that is because they know it to be good if they know what it *is*; it is not their wanting it or their valuing it that makes it good.

Similarly one cannot help but desire happiness (or any good) if one knows what it is. That is what makes John Stuart Mill sound so very foolish when he is trying to establish the value or desirability of happiness as an end (1861: ch. 4). There is no deductive argument, he says, by which we can establish this. And the only non-deductive grounds for claiming that something is desirable is that it is in fact desired. Well, everyone desires happiness, so there must be something in it! If there were not, people would not go on desiring it in the way they do. Those who sample it must know it is the real goods! The truth is that anyone can know happiness to be a good if they know what happiness is; and, unlike ice-cream or Wagner, that does not require having sampled it. But, if we take seriously his claim that his argument is not deductive and ignore his analogy with 'audible' and so forth, at least Mill did not argue that desiring a thing *made* it desirable.[2]

[2]It was C. D. MacNiven who persuaded me to take this claim of Mill's seriously.

98

To sum up. Different people find hedonic value in different things (activities, sensations, experiences, states of affairs). Thus the (hedonic) value of golf, for example is not common. It is nevertheless objective (though subject-dependent) in that it must be discovered in its various objects and is not the creation or product of one's desire or one's will. Further, while different people take pleasure in different things, to take pleasure in a thing is a common as well as an objective value. Nor do we need arguments to determine that pleasure is a good, for that it is a good is more certain than any argument that might be produced in support of it; its goodness (desirability, value, worth) belongs to its nature as a felt quality of experience. So, in the case of hedonic value (pleasure, enjoyment, delight in a thing for its own sake), we have something that (a) is found in different things according to personal taste or preference, (b) is in things (for us) objectively (not created, invented, assigned, or placed there, but *discovered*), (c) is nevertheless subject-dependent, and (d) is a common human good.

It does not follow from any of this that pleasure (enjoying one's activities or experience) is the only inherent or intrinsic personal good. One can find something inherently valuable, or believe it to be inherently valuable, in ways other than that it gives one joy or pleasure or satisfaction, although if one does find it or believe it to be inherently valuable or worthwhile, the attainment of it normally does bring joy or satisfaction. (These matters will be taken up in detail in the next chapter.)

Spinoza held that only what affected the mind could be good or bad (*On the Improvement of the Understanding*, opening sentence), and he thought this sufficient to disprove the objectivity of value (see also 1677: III, 9, note). Spinoza was right in the following respect. Value *is* subject-dependent; there is and could be no value without subjects of experience. But this is perfectly compatible with its objectivity; it does not imply that value is a creation or a product of either desire or the will.

The tables can, in fact, be turned on those who would hold that because there can be no value in a subjectless world, value must be a product or a function of desire or favourable regard. For assume that there can be no value in a world without subjects ('minds'). Nevertheless, of two subjectless worlds proposed to him, a person may favour one over the other, or desire or will the existence of one rather than the other. (This is also to turn the tables on Moore's famous alternative worlds example.) If favouring, or desiring, or willing could create value, then we would have to say that (for him) World 1 had more value than World 2, or that World 1 had value (for him) while World 2 did not. But since both worlds, by hypothesis, contain no subjects, this is impossible. Therefore favouring, desiring, or willing cannot create value, even for the favourer, desirer, or willer.

It is not clear, however, what 'favouring' or 'favourable regard' means here. It could mean simply 'desiring' or 'wanting', or possibly 'preferring', not in the sense of 'liking better', but in the sense of 'desiring more' or 'wanting more', in which case it adds nothing to 'desiring' except the comparative. But it could also be taken to mean 'valuing' or 'regarding as good' or 'regarding as better'. In this respect it resembles the technical term 'pro-attitude', which is supposed to mean both of these things. But we can construct another argument, as follows, to show that valuing or regarding as good is not the same as wanting or willing. For, given that it is incoherent to suppose that there can be value in a subjectless world, it is incoherent to suppose that any such world possesses value (to value it = to think of it as good) or that one such world possesses more value than another, (to value it more = to think of it as better). But it is not incoherent to desire or will one more than the other – to favour or prefer it in that sense. So valuing (regarding as good) is not the same as preferring or favouring where the latter is taken to mean desiring or willing or desiring or willing more strongly.

We can, indeed, construct a third argument, using as a premise the proposition that there can be no value in a subjectless world (that value is subject-dependent), to show that thinking something valuable, i.e. valuing it, cannot make it valuable indeed. For it is perfectly possible to think, incoherently (cf. Moore), that some subjectless world is valuable, or that one such world is more valuable than another. But it is not possible for such a belief to be true. Therefore valuing something cannot make it valuable. Thus the common equation of the subjectivists, desiring = favouring = valuing = being valuable is disproven *using as a premise* the proposition that value is subject-dependent. If desiring = favouring, then favouring ≠ valuing, and it is never the case that valuing = being valuable.

This also indirectly provides the answer to the question whether there are any values that exist not in the world as it is for human beings, but in the world as it (more narrowly) is for human beings of a certain time and place (of a certain culture). I have already said (chapter 3) that whereas to see something as good is to see it as being desirable in respect of its having some desirable character, it is good in reality only if the object actually possesses that character and that character is actually desirable, not merely held or thought to be, in which case it is one of the real forms of (human) good. Now a society may see a thing as good in respect of having a certain character, attribute, or relation. And if we understand how a member of that society sees this as a value, we can understand how he can take it as determining that he has a reason for acting, and hence understand his having some motivational propensity towards having, getting, or doing the thing. But this is not enough to determine that it is a value, i.e. a real good, but only that it is a value within that society in the purely sociological or anthropological sense of the term 'value' i.e. that it is *taken to be* or *regarded as* a value within that society. But, as we have seen, that something is taken to be a value is *not* a sufficient condition of its being one, except, of course, in this purely social-scientific sense.

This conclusion may seem over-hasty and perhaps startling. But it is neither. Cultural relativism is a view that has not been taken seriously by philosophers, Stephen Toulmin possibly excepted (1950: 144–6), until the recent attempts to give it, or to give some form of it, philosophical respectability (Phillips and Mounce 1970; Harman 1975, 1977: 57–133, 1978; Williams 1975). However the sub-Wittgensteinian ('This language-game is played') account of Phillips and Mounce has little credibility, and the arguments of both Harman and Williams are premised on the assumption, now discredited, that no reason can exist for a person unless it relates to his already existing set of desires or motivational propensities.[3]

---

[3]Thus a person can have reason to act as a specific moral principle prescribes only if he/she is a (non-alienated) member of a society which subscribes to it as part of its moral code (Harman 1975, 1977), or an alien value-system cannot be appraised unless it is a 'live option' given the 'concerns' of the culture or group from whose perspective the appraisal is taking place (Williams 1975).

6

Hedonism

In the last two chapters I confined my discussion almost entirely to three kinds of values; hedonic values, values tied to long-range self-interest or one's future well-being (values related to the virtue of prudence), and deontic moral values. However I adverted, from time to time, 'not to be unduly hedonistic' (p. 60), to what persons *otherwise* find inherently valuable or worthwhile (e.g. p. 97), and I argued that prudential and moral values were dependent upon personal values or goods for individuals whatever these should turn out to be.

But was I justified in referring to respects other than those of being pleasant, agreeable, delightful, and so forth, in which a thing can be inherently or intrinsically valuable for an individual person? Is hedonic value perhaps not, ultimately, the only personal value? This is the thesis of hedonism.

We must first consider whether pleasure is to be construed as an inherently desirable subjective state, and whether its opposite – the disagreeable or unpleasant or painful – is to be construed as an inherently undesirable subjective state; whether, in other words, states of pleasure and its opposite are what we have reason to seek or avoid, as the case may be, when our grounds are hedonic, and what it is our aim to achieve, or avoid, when our (rational) motivation is hedonic.

An obvious and familiar answer is that the things we do or seek for pleasure, we seek or do for their own sakes, because we like them. And similarly the things we seek to avoid because of their painful or disagreeable character, we seek to avoid for their own sakes (as it were) because we dislike them; we find them (activities, sensations, experiences, objects of experience) inherently distasteful or disagreeable or unpleasant or distressing in one degree or another (from mildly unpleasant or irritating to acutely painful). But then these characters are felt qualities of the activities, experiences (including sensations), and objects of experience themselves, and logically inseparable from them. In other words we do not seek or seek to avoid these things in order to be in a certain inherently desirable subjective state, namely the pleasant or agreeable, or not to be in a certain inherently undesirable state, namely the painful or unpleasant. Indeed such talk is unintelligible. Enjoying or finding disagreeable some activity, experience, or object of experience, is not reducible to being in a certain identifiable desirable (the pleasant) or undesirable (the unpleasant) state of mind or consciousness or subjectivity, a state that admits of degrees. (This is a mistake attributed to Bentham and, with less force, to J. S. Mill.)

Nevertheless, and in spite of this, there are such things as inherently desirable or undesirable states of consciousness or subjective being. These are characterized by what, on the positive side, is called, in the United States and Canada, 'feeling good', and, in Britain, 'being in good spirits', and, on the negative side, 'feeling depressed' or being 'down in the dumps', or 'feeling miserable'. There is a continuum of such states, ranging from feeling on top of the world, or 'feeling great', as Americans and Canadians say, to suicidal despair, and at any time anyone's state of spirits can be located somewhere along this continuum. Such states can be caused by beliefs and perceptions (e.g. that one has won a lot of money, that someone close to one has died), and they can take an intentional object (often the content of the belief that is the cause). Thus they can be, e.g. *about* one's prospects for a job, *about* the world situation, *that* someone close to one has died, *that* one has won the race, and so forth. But they may be caused by hormonal change, by drugs, by changes in the weather, or the cause need not be known at all.

Notice, however, that such states are not to be identified with pleasure and pain, though they are perhaps close to what Spinoza meant by '*laetitia*' and '*tristitia*' ('joy' and 'sorrow', sometimes mistranslated as 'pleasure' and 'pain') (1677: II, 11, note). For pleasure and pain are found *in things* (activities, experiences, objects of experience) and are logically inseparable from those things, of which they are a felt quality, whereas being in good or in low spirits (feeling good or feeling depressed), whether or not one is aware of the cause and whether or not they take an intentional object, are isolable states of consciousness or of being. Further they are causally related to pleasure and its opposite, in both directions, for feeling good can increase one's capacity for pleasure, and doing what one

103

likes doing can make one feel better than one did before.

A possible version of hedonism would be the doctrine that the inherently desirable subjective state of feeling good was the only end worth pursuing, and that a rational person, when seeking good for himself or herself, would seek to feel as good as possible, or to maintain a state as high as possible on the continuum, over as long a time as possible. (On this view, being in poor or in low spirits would be the only evil.) But such a view is easily refuted, partly because certain activities, experiences, and objects of experience are delightful in themselves, hence valuable, hence rational to seek for their own sakes and not as a means to some further end, and partly because euphoria (the highest degree of feeling good) can be induced by drugs, by hypnosis, or by electrical stimulation of the brain, in which case the highest human good would be to have our central nervous systems continuously maintained in a certain state, while we remain passive – a view which I think no one, except perhaps the fakir lying on his bed of nails and staring at the sun, would be prepared to accept. A more acceptable hedonism – the kind I shall consider – is the view that the good for a person consists in his doing (experiencing) as much as possible of what he likes doing (experiencing), and as little as possible of what he dislikes. And, of course, this will involve normal perception, knowledge (or true belief), and the capacity for action. Pleasure and its opposite, except perhaps in the case of sensations, involve contact with, and agency in, the world around us. They are not, properly understood, unlike feeling good and its opposite, simply inherently desirable or undesirable states of consciousness or felt being.

Mill makes the issue very simple indeed. To desire anything for its own sake, moral virtue included, just is to think of it as pleasurable. They are one and the same thing (Mill 1861: ch. 4). Desire aims at satisfaction (second sense) and satisfaction just is pleasure. Since desire aims at the good (the desirable), intrinsic or inherent value consists in satisfaction. (If this interpretation is correct, Mill's view is a version of the kind of restricted hedonism mentioned on p. 45 above.)

There are a number of things that can be seen to be wrong here, in the light of what has been argued to this point. It is only reflective desire, and not appetite or inclination, that aims at the good. Appetite and inclination certainly aim at *their* satisfaction, but this is satisfaction in the first, not in the second sense. So the question of what is good cannot be settled by determining what it is that desire aims at (Aristotle to the contrary notwithstanding). Mill would have to argue (as, indeed, he sometimes appears to do) that to *think of something as good* and to think of it as pleasurable were one and the same, that one could not think of something as inherently or intrinsically good except by thinking of it as pleasurable. But that is straightforwardly false. One can think of something's being intrinsically good in respect of its being *noble*, for example. In thinking of something as intrinsically good, one is not required to think of it as good in respect of being agreeable. It could still be true that pleasure was the only good, but one could no longer argue that this was necessarily so, anything else being (literally) unthinkable.

Jan Narveson, the only important contemporary hedonist of whom I am aware, argues, in apparently similar vein, that what he calls 'psychological hedonism' is trivially true, because to take pleasure in a thing just is to regard it, when sampled, as intrinsically good, so that coming to regard a thing as intrinsically valuable or worthwhile is the very same thing as discovering that it gives pleasure, enjoyment, or satisfaction:

It turns out that 'pleasure and the absence of pain', after all the qualifications, interpolations, and interpretations are in, means 'whatever it is that people seek for its own sake when they are rational'; which is equivalent, in turn, to 'that by reference to which people appraise courses of action' ('naturally', i.e. apart from moral considerations); which is, in turn, tautologically, what they regard as intrinsically good (1967: 66).

It is interesting that Narveson should call this 'psychological' hedonism. Of course it is true that we are all in the habit, ingrained for more than a century, of dividing hedonism into the psychological and the ethical, the former being the view that only pleasure *is* pursued, the latter being the view that only pleasure *should* be pursued. And since we are not dealing with morality here, it must be psychological hedonism that is in question, so we are inclined to suppose. But we can, in fact, make at least the following *six* distinctions. (1) Only pleasure is desired. (2) People are motivated only by *considerations* of pleasure. (3) Only pleasure is thought to be intrinsically good. (4) Only pleasure is *rationally* sought. (5) Only pleasure is intrinsically good. (6) One morally ought to seek pleasure and only to seek pleasure.

Narveson restricts ethical hedonism to (6), leaving everything else in the realm of psychological hedonism. But the expression 'psychological hedonism' applies properly only to (1) and (2), that is if psychological hedonism is to be understood as a theory of *motivation*. (4) might also be thought to belong to motivation theory, but when one speaks of what is *rationally* sought, in the sense of what is sought *with reason*, motivation theory spills over into axiology, since reasons that *ground* actions are logically tied to values (This involves the ambiguity discussed on pp. 29–30 above.)

It is not clear how one would make out a case for the truth of (1). Mill (1861: ch. 4) merely affirms it. But however we interpret it, as an empirical or as some kind of necessary truth, it is certainly false. Mill claims that to desire something for its own sake is to desire it for pleasure and that reflection will show that it cannot be otherwise! But this, if it is not stipulation, is mere dogma. Some do desire for its own sake, e.g. virtue, and *not* because it is perceived as agreeable or pleasant. (2) is false because it assumes that all acts are rationally motivated, but some acts (as we have seen) are not motivated by *considerations*, i.e. by the belief that one has a reason and the desire consequent upon this, at all. Narveson is claiming of (3) and (4) that they are tautologically true, with just a hint of (5), but later (1967: 84) he quite specifically denies (5), granting that things other than satisfactions might be intrinsically good in some sense, but that this would be irrelevant to ethics. In any case it is plain that (5) can be classified neither as psychological nor as ethical hedonism. If we must give it a name, we can call it 'axiological hedonism'. It is the matter at present under discussion.

The view, like (1) attributable to Mill,[1] which I attempted to refute at the beginning of the chapter, was that (5) was true *because* (3) was true. This is only going to work as an argument if (3) is to be

[1] Both of these views are attributable to Mill on the basis of the same passage, namely: 'And now to decide whether ... mankind do desire nothing for itself but that which is a pleasure to them, or of which the absence is a pain, we have evidently arrived at a question of fact and experience, dependent, like all similar questions, upon evidence. It can only be determined by practiced self-consciousness and self-observation, assisted by observation of others. I believe that these sources of evidence, impartially consulted, will declare that desiring a thing and finding it pleasant, aversion to it and thinking of it as painful, are phenomena entirely inseparable or, rather, two parts of the same phenomenon – in strictness of language, two different modes of naming the same psychological fact; that to think of an object as desirable (unless for the sake of its consequences) and to think of it as pleasant are one and the same thing; and that to desire anything except in proportion as the idea of it is pleasant is a physical and metaphysical impossibility' (1861: 49).

understood in the sense that it would be *incoherent* to think of anything besides pleasure (the agreeable) as good because to think of something as inherently good and to think of it as pleasurable or agreeable are one and the same thing. The refutation of this argument consists in noting that not only do people think of things as intrinsically good in respect of being, e.g., noble or pure, understood as quite distinct from their being pleasurable or agreeable, but that there is nothing self-contradictory or incoherent in any way about their so thinking. Pleasure might still be the only good, but then these opinions (e.g. that something was intrinsically good in respect of being pure) would have to be false on grounds other than their supposed incoherence. What Mill is essentially arguing for is a conceptual identity between 'intrinsically pleasurable' and 'intrinsically worthwhile'. But in the natural language no such conceptual identity exists; therefore to state that there is one is either an (ignorable) stipulation or it is false. The concept of pleasure or of the agreeable has a real empirical content; it is not just whatever anyone finds, in respect of whatever quality, instrinsically worthwhile. Axiological hedonism is not self-evidently true.

It is interesting that Narveson identifies (3) with (4). On the view that I have been advocating, if (4) were true, then (5) would necessarily follow, if 'rationally' is interpreted as 'with rational grounding', for that would mean, since reasons grounding an action exist only where something of value is to be gained, that pleasure is the only value. But this is not what Narveson means. What he means is that, where they are seeking for themselves what has inherent value, the only *reason* for the sake of which people act is the prospect of pleasure (or the prospect of pleasure covers all possible reasons); otherwise they act without a reason, or do not act rationally. Thus his (4) is equivalent to (3) on the assumption that one believes oneself to have a reason for doing something only in respect of believing that something of worth is to be accomplished, that something good or desirable is to be gained.

It is by identifying (4) with (3) that Narveson is able (as he supposes) to escape the move from (4) to (5). And because he confines his self-evident or tautological hedonism to (3) and (4), taken as equivalent, the label 'psychological hedonism' does not seem too out of place. But in spite of his denials, which are half-hearted and intended mainly as a sop to intuitionists, he is really an axiological hedonist at heart. Mill's equation is: to think of something as pleasant = to think of it as desirable (good). And from this conceptual identity there follows the equation: what is pleasant = what is good. Narveson's equation is: pleasure = what is *regarded as* (thought to be, believed to be) intrinsically good. And, as he well knows, a thing's being *thought* to be intrinsically good is perfectly consistent with its *not* being intrinsically good (sop to the intuitionists).

The trouble is that enjoying a thing or finding it pleasant or agreeable, or finding that one likes it, is a *discovery* of value. Hedonic value is something that is recognized in its being experienced. It is a felt quality of certain activities, sensations, and other experiences. Therefore, in enjoying something one does not regard it as intrinsically worthwhile, one *experiences* it as intrinsically worthwhile. To make Narveson's equation coherent we are forced to revise it to read: pleasure (the pleasant) = what is found (discovered) to be intrinsically good. But, given that a good must at least in principle be recognizable as such by the person for whom it is a good – a position I have been advocating all along, and one upon which Narveson himself lays heavy emphasis – this is a full-fledged axiological hedonism. By having 'pleasure' on one side of his equation, rather than 'thought pleasant', and 'thought good' rather than 'good' on the other, Narveson is able to disguise his axiological hedonism, to which he is strongly committed, as a psychological hedonism only, and further one that is only tautologically or trivially true.

And how is he able to manage this conjuring trick? First, he plays upon the ambiguity in 'rational' between 'rationally motivated' and 'rationally grounded'. Second, and relatedly, he falls back upon the non-cognitivists' concept of a 'pro-attitude'. Like Patrick Nowell-Smith (1954: 111–12) and others, Narveson throws into one basket such diverse things as wanting, desiring, valuing, preferring, liking, enjoying, and labels the basket 'pro-attitudes'. But there are three importantly different kinds of thing in this basket: (1) wanting or desiring which, as we have seen, has no implications either for valuing (regarding as desirable) or for value, (2) valuing or regarding as good, which is consistent with the thing valued or regarded as good not being good in reality, and (3) liking or enjoying or finding pleasant or agreeable, which is a kind of experiencing of value.

What Narveson does is to rely on the assumed identity of (2) and (3), which gives his equation whatever plausibility it has, while at the same he treats (2) as a case of (1) only, leaving actual intrinsic value – supposing there is such a thing – to the intuitionists to go play with in their back yard, if they want to. In fact, of course, Narveson is claiming that the only real, substantial, recognizable, experienced (not airy-fairy, pie-in-the-sky, Platonic) value is *liking* or *enjoying* a thing. But instead of saying this directly, he attempts to defuse it by identifying it with (3) – valuing or supposing to be valuable. Note that we have here a real blood-and-guts hedonism, not a trivial tautology, as Narveson makes it out to be. The supposed tautology could only result from a claimed identity between 'good' or 'desirable' and 'pleasant' or 'agreeable', a view already rejected in connection with Mill. Note that Mill can be construed as saying that 'the pleasant' is just another name for 'the good' or 'the desirable', whatever that should turn out to be, so placing no restriction whatever on the content of the desirable. Narveson represents himself as a follower of Mill in this respect, but whereas Mill's is a bloodless and ghostly hedonism, Narveson's is not. Narveson *does* wish to restrict the content of the intrinsically valuable; it is confined to what one likes or finds agreeable, disguised as whatever one happens to regard as intrinsically valuable. We are being offered the blood and guts in, as it were, pale and ghostly clothing.

Furthermore, as Narveson has expressed it, his account contains one glaring error that is shared with Mill. For if there is a conceptual (or other necessary) identity between the pleasant and what one *regards as* intrinsically good or desirable, this implies that (in some sense of the word) 'pleasant' is, of necessity, the only character in respect of which one regards a thing as desirable – 'pleasant' is the only desirability characteristic, or the universal one under which all others are subsumed. But, as I have already said, people can see things as being intrinsically good or desirable in respect of being noble or pure (to take just two examples) and it is difficult to see how these could be subsumed under the pleasant in *any* sense of the word.

Or perhaps 'liking' and 'finding pleasant', in a broad sense, are to be taken as *synonyms* for 'valuing for its own sake' or 'regarding as intrinsically good'. In that case, 'being pleasant' or 'being agreeable' would not itself be a desirability characterization, but a thing would have to be liked or found pleasant (= valued) in respect of possessing some further desirable character. But this formula is clearly wrong. We *value* a thing in respect of its possessing some (supposedly) desirable character, but we *like*, correctly speaking, some aspect of a thing which is not normally itself a desirability character. Thus what I value about a certain brand of beer is its pleasant or agreeable taste (desirability character), but what I *like* about it is its taste, simply. And while there is nothing at all wrong with saying that one values a thing in respect of its nobility or its purity, it would be very odd indeed to say that, as a matter of personal taste, one *liked* that aspect of it. Being personally liked is one kind of desirability characterization; being noble or pure is another kind altogether.

On the revised formula, however – the pleasant = what is *found* to be good – the belief that purity and nobility are (independent) forms of goodness can be rejected as error – as mere Platonic hoo-ha. Pleasure is a felt quality of activities and experiences. It is a value experienced immediately. But the noble? the pure? They belong with the chaste in the ancient-and-medieval wastebasket. It is certainly true, in any case, as I have already argued, that to regard a certain character as desirable does not ensure that it is so. The original equation – thought desirable = pleasant – would make it logically impossible to regard a character as desirable when in fact it was not (though only one thing *could* be thought desirable, namely the pleasant or agreeable). So let us agree to correct Narveson on this point and ponder the more plausible identity – is enjoyable = is found to be inherently worthwhile.

We are concerned here, as elsewhere, with values as they relate to practical reason, values as they determine that reasons for action exist, which can be recognized as such by agents and used by them in their deliberations. We are concerned, then, with values for the sake of which a rational agent acts or can act. If we are to say that pleasure is the only value, in that to find, or discover, or recognize intrinsic value just is to discover that one *likes* something (undisguised Narvesonian axiological hedonism), then we are saying that rational agents (agents whose acts are both rationally motivated and rationally grounded) will only act in order to get what they like, or to avoid what they dislike, unless their reasons are moral; or, in other words, unless they are acting on moral grounds, hedonic value is the only value they will pursue. (This is only a way of saying, of course, that hedonic value is the only thing *that one has reason* to pursue for oneself. The point is axiological, not psychological.)

It was supposed to be one of the great advantages, for utilitarians and others, of the want-satisfaction theory of value or, for those who wish to avoid mention of value, of the want-satisfaction theory of what it is rational to seek (what one has reason to seek), that, unlike hedonism, which restricted the good to pleasure and the avoidance of pain, it placed no restriction at all on the *content* of anyone's good; what was good for a person (what it was rational for him to pursue) was what he desired and that was that, the good being realized in the satisfaction of the want, whatever that happened to be. True, there were some things that *everybody* wanted, such as liberty, the means of subsistence, protection from evils, etc., hence these things were common goods, but otherwise goodness was entirely a matter of what every individual happened to desire. One would have expected Narveson, as the best, completest, and most systematic of the latter-day defenders of utilitarianism, to conform to this pattern and, indeed, one has the feeling that he would certainly *like* to. Furthermore he does, like so many others (as I have already noted), lump desires and wants, together with valuations, preferences, and likings, under the heading 'pro-attitudes' (Narveson 1967: 89–90). Yet he acknowledges that one can have desires that one does *not* regard as providing good reasons for acting, that we can have desires that we acknowledge to be (inherently) bad ones. But he argues that we can assume, unless the agent himself tells us otherwise, that he positively values the objects of his desires. 'It is for this reason that we will, in general, assume that what a person enjoys, what pleases him, or what he prefers, likes, wants, desires, etc., are likewise measures of utility' (Narveson 1967: 90).

Here is an instance of the 'lumping' just adverted to. Desiring or wanting is here equated with enjoying, being pleased by, and liking, even in a context where it is being admitted that one need not value the objects of one's desires, and just after the thesis that enjoying, being pleased by, or liking something is *the same as* supposing it to have intrinsic value (valuing it) has been adumbrated. Thus we observe the almost hypnotic influence of the non-cognitivists' concept of a 'pro-attitude'! If Narveson is to be inconsistent, however, let us introduce consistency on his behalf: to desire or want an object is one thing; to regard it as valuable is another. (Narveson's claim that valuing a thing, or regarding it as intrinsically good, is the same as being pleased by it is the one we have just examined and found wanting. We have already made, on his behalf, the necessary correction in that regard.) So, in the end, Narveson (or the corrected Narveson) is not a want-satisfaction theorist but a hedonist and, unlike Mill, a real one too. A thing has intrinsic value for a person if and only if it is liked, or he or she enjoys it, or is pleased by or with it. And rational agents (persons whose actions are grounded by reasons), except when they are acting on moral grounds, act only for the sake of having, getting, or doing what pleases them (and avoiding or getting rid of what displeases them). This is the view we must now examine.

There is one sense of the words 'hedonism' and 'hedonist' that Narveson denies that his kind of (as he claims, tautological, but as we now know, substantive) hedonism has anything to do with, namely hedonism as it is associated with 'the life of pleasure' – single-hearted devotion to 'the good things of life' when one is acting on other than moral grounds (1967: 52–3). And Narveson makes this denial on the ground that this represents just one kind of taste or preference. (He recognizes that 'pleasure' does have this narrower sense.) The reason he rejects this form of hedonism and denies utterly that it has anything to do with utilitarianism is that this particular kind of pleasure might not happen to be the favourite of just anyone. The business executive who devotes seventy hours a week to his work and the fakir who spends his whole time on his bed of nails and (or?) contemplating his navel, may also be doing *what they like to do*, what they find pleasing or enjoyable – though it is not pleasure in the narrower sense of the term. Utilitarianism, and hence Narveson's hedonism, most importantly permits everyone to do his or her own thing. And one's own thing needn't be the life of pleasure (hedonism as a way of life) in the narrow sense. One need not be a person who devotes his or her life to yachts, villas, parties, food, wine, sex, games, entertainments and diversions or, if one is not rich, the same sort of thing on a lesser scale. One may be more given to beds of nails, working in the lab or office sixteen hours a day, living naked in caves, or attending to the needs of lepers, i.e. these things may *please* one more. Of course one cannot *condemn* the hedonistic (in the narrow sense) life; if that is one's thing, then that is one's thing. Utilitarianism, hence Narveson's hedonism, is (importantly) neutral on these matters, just as the want-satisfaction theory is.

There is a sense, then, in which every rational agent (= agent whose actions are grounded in reasons) except when restricted by moral consideration, devotes himself or herself to the pursuit of pleasure, namely the pursuit of *whatever he or she likes for its own sake*. However, there is another sense in which he or she does not, unless, by chance, attracted to eating, drinking, yachting, and so forth (pleasure in the narrow sense) as a full-time or maximum possible time proposition and, by implication, there are many who are not attracted to that kind of life. For them the 'life of pleasure' would be a dreadful bore. And that is not because they prefer good books, classical music, or elevated conversation; hedonism (narrow sense) need not be *vulgar* hedonism. Indeed Narveson actually says: 'A business executive who devoted all of his time to his work, seventy hours a week, and professed either to have no time for, or no interest in, the arts, good food, interesting company, and so forth, would not naturally be classed as a hedonist [narrow sense]' (1967: 52). And among the typical interests of this kind of hedonist he mentions, in addition to these, music (specifically among the arts), women (no doubt the hedonist he has in mind is male), sports, and conversation.

It should be apparent that what these things have in common is not that they constitute the interests or a disjunction of the interests of a certain kind of person, namely the (narrow) hedonist, but that they are all things that we do when we are taking time off, when we do not have (for the nonce) a job of work to do, what we may do all the time (to all intents and purposes) when we are *on holiday*. In general they are the things that we do when we are *at leisure*. They are leisure-time activities. If you should doubt me, look at the list again: the arts, good food, interesting company, the opposite sex, sports, conversation. And it is plainly not either practicing the arts or engaging in sports as a professional that Narveson is talking about, but as a spectator, viewer, reader, or listener or, if a participant, as an amateur – in any case sports or the arts as a leisure-time pursuit. And as well as the things mentioned, all recreations and amusements will be on the list, indeed all the things that, as we say, are *done for pleasure*. These things belong on the leisure side of the common distinction between work and leisure, on the pleasure side of the common distinction between business and pleasure.

The life of pleasure, therefore, does not exhibit a special kind of taste or preference or liking (to be contrasted with beds of nails and so forth), but is a life devoted entirely to leisure-time activities, a life which requires some means of support other than labour, a life which is, in an important sense, *idle*, a life which is often regarded as wasteful and, if very sucessful, luxurious and extravagant – often enough morally depraved. We find this character under various names and guises: the wastrel, prodigal, good-for-nothing, sponger, gold-digger, playboy, gigolo, parasite, lounge lizard, jet-setter, sybarite, beautiful person, and so forth. The important thing about this person is that he or she *does nothing* (in a sense), because he or she is always at leisure. The rest of us are, of course, free some of the time to do things for pleasure, but for a large part of the time we must keep our noses to the grindstone. That we do something for pleasure is, of course, no guarantee that we will in fact enjoy it. And the life dedicated to pleasure is very likely to turn into a tedious bore. But we may only *seek* it, in any case, when we are at leisure – this is a tautology – in our leisure-time, off-hours, or holiday activities, in the moments, hours, days, or weeks (possibly lifetimes) when we are free from the cares or necessities of work or business.

This sort of activity (doing things for pleasure) is contrasted with that whereby either one labours and toils for some reward, or one engages in some project which one regards as having worth, whether that worth lies in its being a means to the achievement of some worthwhile end, or is inherently or intrinsically valuable or worthwhile in some sense other than that it entertains me, diverts me, keeps me from boredom, or gives me pleasure. In either case this is work, not leisure; business, not pleasure. And that is not to say that I may not *take pleasure in it*. If I am lucky I will enjoy my work, and I will enjoy it still more if I see it as accomplishing something of value or worth, a value or worth that cannot be identified with the pleasure I take in it. What I am now doing as I write this is work, work that is unquestionably toilsome, but which I am nevertheless able to enjoy, not when the work is slow and knotted and difficult, but when I believe I have uncovered something, made a discovery, or when I feel that I am getting somewhere. I am also persuaded that philosophy is inherently worth doing in some sense other than that I like doing philosophy.

And here is the crux of the matter. There is a sense, Narveson tells us, in which, moral reasons aside, everything a rational agent (here = agent who is rationally motivated and for whom what he thinks are reasons really are reasons) does, he does for pleasure, and that is that he seeks only what pleases him or what he likes, which need not be limited to any particular set of objects, activities, or experiences – everyone to his or her own taste. But it has turned out, on examination, that this amounts to nothing but what one does *for pleasure*, in the common acceptation of that term. Narveson's attempt to distinguish the narrow hedonist from the broad hedonist has failed, since narrow hedonist pursuits have turned out to be not a limited class of things liked (things like by certain persons), such as agreeable sensations, but to include all leisure-time pursuits, and these now turn out to be just those things that one does (seeks, pursues, keeps) solely because one likes them. And this would apply even to the business executive who devoted seventy hours a week to his 'work', given that he did it for pleasure alone!

The doctrine might still be saved if it could be argued that work or business was always drudgery – burdensome labour undertaken in order, first of all, to ensure survival and, after that, to provide income for beer, amusement, and hobbies. The theory could survive, in other words, if the labourer saw no worth in his or her labour other than its giving him the means for staying alive and for keeping him entertained and jollified. No doubt many lives are like this, but it is *unfortunate* that this is so; it is not the ideal. Ideally a man or a woman's *work* should be a contribution to his or her happiness or fulfilment. But if it is work and she is not at leisure, then she is doing it for something other than pleasure, for some reason other than that she likes doing it, for the accomplishment of some end other than her private enjoyment or satisfaction. (That she *derives* pleasure or satisfaction from her work is not really relevant, since she is not acting *for the sake of it*.) What we have here are supposed grounding reasons for action tied to ends (things valued for their own sakes) whose perceived value cannot be boiled down to the agent's liking or enjoying them or to pleasure in *any* sense of that term.

And, so it seems, the best-off, happiest people, are those who are able to find some degree of fulfilment in their work, in the things that they do for reasons other than that they like or enjoy doing them, these latter things being, by definition, their leisure-time activities. And we may compare their lives favourably with those who endure burdensome drudgery only so as to be able to pay for their subsistence and their fun. The happiest people, then, are those who *value for their own sakes* things in some respect *other* than that they like them or enjoy them, or that they occupy their time pleasantly or agreeably. Bread and circuses may keep the rabble quiet, but they do not fulfil a woman or a man. He or she must have some work to do, not just to have his bread and circuses, but which (or the end of which) he can value for its own sake. And being work, not leisure, he must value it in some respect other than that it affords him pleasure or amusement. Indeed, if one is to do one's job well, one must be devoted to it. If one acts as if one were at leisure when one is on the job, that will ensure that the job is not done properly, since one will not do anything – unless forced to it – that one does not see some pleasure or amusement in doing, and certainly nothing that seems burdensome. When one is engaged in a job or a project, one must aim at doing the job or completing the project, and not at one's pleasure or amusement, which is irrelevant. If one is to be motivated to *do the job* or complete the project, one must value its end. Otherwise one simply does what one *has* to do (with heavy supervision, to prevent slacking) in order to win one's bread and one's circus tickets.

But in spite of all this, hedonism could still be true. We have seen that aspects of things other than their being agreeable or being liked *are* valued for their own sakes, and indeed that the happiest and best-off people do value things for their own sakes in respect of something other than that they are liked or enjoyed or privately preferred. But because a thing is valued for its own sake, it does not follow that it is genuinely valuable, even for the valuer. The belief that something is good or worthwhile can be mistaken. Thus it could be that pleasure and only pleasure (objects, activities, and experiences in respect of being enjoyable or being liked) was intrinsically valuable, desirable, or good, and that all those who believed otherwise, who thought there was something in work as well as in leisure, were deluded, even if they were happier. We would have to argue that their greater happiness was a consequence of their delusion! We could envy their greater happiness, but as rational men and women, knowing that pleasure is the only thing worth seeking, we could never have it! We would have to argue that, given their false beliefs, these people were rationally motivated, but that their behaviour was rationally quite ungrounded. This would be a kind of happiness that a truly enlightened and rational man or woman could neither seek nor hope for.

This should already be enough to make us suspicious. But note that these people are not *pursuing* pleasure. The pleasure, fulfilment, happiness, that they derive from their jobs is gratuitous; it is not sought for. If it was pleasure or enjoyment that was being sought, then these would not be jobs of work but leisure-time activities. Jobs of work of necessity prescribe a certain direction to one's activities without regard to what one would choose for pleasure.

And so we cannot take the easy way out and say that whatever has value for a person, so providing him or her with reasons for action, other than (the prospect of) pleasure, is whatever brings happiness and fulfilment, for it can only *bring* happiness and fulfilment if it is valued (thought to be valuable) in some other respect. The happiness and fulfilment is a value all right, but it is one that one can only achieve, as it were indirectly, by aiming at something, not because it is a means to happiness and fulfilment, but for the sake of some *other* value it is thought to possess. It might still be true that there was no such value, that personal happiness was all. But that our situation is *so* ironic is not a conclusion to be accepted lightly.

Happiness and fulfilment depend upon the belief that one's life is itself worthwhile in the sense of being meaningful or significant, that it matters somehow, that it makes a difference. All of this is irritatingly vague, but nothing is a greater bar to happiness, a greater cause of depression, cynicism, and despair, than the belief that it all counts for nothing, that in the end it does not matter at all. And the mere having of pleasant or agreeable experiences, together with the avoidance of unpleasant and disagreeable ones, is not enough to give one the sense that one's life and one's activities are meaningful or significant.

An old-fashioned utilitarian might say that what is missing in this person's life is doing anything, or engaging in any project, beyond his or her strict obligations, that will increase the amount of pleasure in the world, other than his or her own, and decrease the amount of 'pain'. If a person is to be happy, he or she must do something for others beyond what justice strictly requires. He recognizes the value of happiness for others equally with his own, and if he does nothing beyond the call of duty to increase the happiness or decrease the misery of others, he suffers from a sense of guilt or shame or inadequacy. A modern utilitarian might say that the man or woman is aware that he or she is, strict obligation aside, not doing anything to add to the want-satisfactions or to decrease the want-frustrations of the other people in the world. He or she will not be happy unless they see themselves as making a contribution to the well-being of society by *producing* something – goods or services – that will cater to some wants, or prevent, remove, or alleviate some things that other people want to avoid. A Narvesonian utilitarian might diagnose the situation as one in which the person, while doing what morality requires of him, is discontented, because he is doing nothing to make it possible for others to engage in activities that they value for their own sakes (= like), or in avoiding other things that they dislike.

On all these accounts, there is still only one intrinsic value (or, in Narveson's case, only one thing to be *treated* as an intrinsic value), whether it is pleasure, want-satisfaction, or getting (having, doing) what one likes. It is just that we should be spreading the joy around a little bit, instead of hoarding it for ourselves, and not just when morality *requires* some sacrifice. It is essentially a case of *selfishness*. The reason the waster feels so rotten (if he does) is that he is not being a useful citizen (as the cant phrase has it); he is not making his contribution to the social economy, which means, in the end, producing more pleasure (and less pain), or more want-satisfactions (and less want-frustrations) or more things done (had, gotten, kept) because they are fancied for their own sakes.

But this account of the matter will not do. It is true that one of the things that can give one a sense of the worth of one's own life, its meaningfulness or significance, is that one is doing something to serve others or to serve society – providing a product or a service from which others benefit, which makes the world a better place to live in, at least for some people, than it would be otherwise. The understanding that one is, in this sense, a useful member of society does aid one's self-esteem and the sense that one's life is valuable or significant. And making the world a better place to live in could be understood in terms of more pleasure and less unpleasantness, more for people of what they like and less of what they dislike (though not, for reasons already expressed at length, more of what they want and less of what they want to avoid).

But there is a vital ingredient missing, and that is precisely the conception of something's having a value or a worth, determining that one has reason to pursue it, quite independently of its either being, or being a means to, something agreeable for some person (or the prevention, removal, or lessening of something disagreeable). If it all boils down simply to having as much of a good time as possible and as little of a bad time, whether for myself or for humankind in general, then it seems, if not exactly frivolous, wanting in weight, significance, or importance. There are things to aim at that are finer, more noble, more meaningful than pleasure, whether it be mine or someone else's. One need not do a hero's deeds, but one must develop one's particular skills and talents, realize one's potential (or try to), and perhaps also one must serve some ideal of goodness or value beyond or distinct from that of maximizing (utilitarianism) or justly distributing (Rawls) the satisfactions of economic man, the want-machine.

All of this will be seen by the hardened hedonist or want-satisfaction theorist as just so much Platonic, or intuitionist, or worse, Nietzschean hoo-ha. It will also be seen as dangerous, since idealism can certainly go wrong, and the following of such ideals as patriotism, racial purity, or the one true religion, has led to some of the greatest social evils in history. And every civilized and rational person knows that massive human suffering can never be justified by the pursuit of such ideals. Nor is the great artist permitted to trample on the rights of others in order to ensure the greatest flowering of his talents. Such views are evil, and we all know them to be so. The answer to this difficulty in general is that, *contra* Nietzsche, deontic moral requirements bind us all to have regard for certain of the interests of others, and especially not to cause them harm, so no ideal can take precedence over the claims of deontic morality. And if an ideal, e.g. racial purity, is such that it cannot, in principle, help but conflict with deontic moral claims, which are universalist by nature, then it must be rejected as a false ideal, one not worthy of being sought.

But within the restrictions placed on us by deontic moral considerations (considerations of moral requirement or necessity), there are things to be chosen by us *for ourselves* on grounds other than that we like them or they please us, or that they are the means to something that we like or that pleases us. *Contra* Narveson, we can value things for their own sakes in respect of their possessing many characters, by no means all of them reducible to or subsumable under being pleasant, agreeable, or liked. (Two examples are purity and nobility.) Nor, when we value something in respect of its being noble or pure, is this properly glossed as a case of *liking* it or finding it pleasing *in respect of* its being noble or pure.

But the revised, neo-Narvesonian hedonistic formula is different. No longer is *valuing* something intrinsically the same as liking it, but liking it is the same as finding or discovering it to be valuable intrinsically. And there's the rub. For hedonic value, and seemingly only hedonic value, is *experienced as valuable*, so that no question of its value can be raised. If I enjoy something, the judgment that it has at least this value for me is incorrigible. It is an actual tasting of value, if you like. Pleasure is a value that is actually experienced; nobility and purity are not. Nor can we be certain what possesses nobility or purity, nor even that these things are indeed values, though they are certainly respects in which things are thought (by some) to be valuable or worthy of pursuit or attainment. We can find out if a thing is pleasant (or unpleasant or neutral) by sampling it. But this seems to be true of no other kind of value. Is it only in respect of being pleasant or liked, then, that a thing can be found or discovered, in this direct way, to have intrinsic value? Here is the strongest case for hedonism. However, I have just spoken (by implication) not only of nobility and purity as genuine values to be pursued, but also of developing one's talents, trying to realize one's potential, and things in general more *significant* than the mere pursuit of what one likes (and avoidance of what one dislikes). How can one make out a case for such things being values?

There is another way in which this problem can be approached. On the hedonist view, a person's good consists in his getting as much as possible of what he likes, and as little as possible of what he dislikes, over as long a time as possible, with preference given to getting (having, keeping) what one likes the most, and avoiding (lessening, getting rid of) what one dislikes the most. On the alternative picture, which I am advocating, this is inadequate. At least part of a person's good, on the view I am putting forward, consists in one's *making* something of oneself, in having projects whose motivation to complete is not based on how much working on it is liked or enjoyed or found pleasant, but whose end, rather, is seen to have some intrinsic or inherent worth of its own. Whether one's job essentially consists in providing, or helping to provide, a product or a service for others, thus satisfying an already existing demand, or whether one is creating something of novel worth, there is always, minimally, the value of *doing one's job well*, which permits, e.g. the craftsman to take pride in his workmanship or indeed, as we say, in the *quality* of his workmanship. There is an inherent worth in fulfilling one's task, supposing it to have value, to the best of one's ability, and the case of various skills and talents, *striving after excellence.* The members of the European Community Youth Symphony Orchestra, whom I saw and heard playing recently, were not seeking their own pleasure, nor were they aiming, in a calculating, prudential way, to display their talents before any agents of potential future employers who might be present, and who might then provide them with bread and butter and extra pocket-money for going to discos at night. They cared about what they were doing and they were trying to do their best. Furthermore their so doing was rationally justified. And – just in case it had not been noted – they were not at leisure but very much on the job.

A vital ingredient that is missing from the hedonistic picture (intrinsic value consists simply in what people like and the absence of what they dislike) is the kind of value that commands or merits *respect* in addition to constituting a reward or pay-off. If a person has a lot of what she likes and little of what she dislikes over a long period of time, we may say she is well off and we may envy her, but there is nothing about her yet which gives her any special worth as a person, which commands, inspires, or indeed merits special respect, including self-respect. And this is to ignore a dimension of value which simply cannot be ignored. In the most general, and the most ancient, sense of the term, what is missing is virtue, or excellence. And this will include not only the development and exercise of a person's particular talents, and some contribution to the well-being of the community, but also the whole range of *moral* virtue, which is what makes a person good in respect of being a human being, whatever that should turn out to be (though it will obviously include such things as courage, prudence, honesty, and self-control).

Virtue, in this broad sense, is not simply a means to the production of a certain end-state for some person or persons, but is itself something to be pursued for its own sake, for it is virtue and only virtue – this is a necessary truth – that gives us special worth as persons, i.e. whatever worth we have in addition to the worth that everyone has simply in respect of being a person. And if we do not have special worth as persons, while we may be blameless, we merit no rewards. And knowing or believing this, though we may find much enjoyment in life, we are quite incapable of happiness or fulfilment. We cannot be happy unless we endeavour to be good; mere pleasure-seeking cannot lead to happiness. We have reason, therefore, first to strive for excellence and only then to seek pleasure.

7

Good and evil

It can surely be agreed that just as enjoying a thing (activity, experience, object of experience) is inherently good or desirable (hedonic value), so finding an activity, experience, or object of experience unpleasant or disagreeable or painful (as distinct from merely *not* desirable) is inherently bad or evil or undesirable (negative hedonic value); also that feeling depressed or in poor or low spirits is an inherently undesirable subjective state, just as feeling good or being in good spirits is an inherently desirable one.

That there is something inherently bad or undesirable or evil about having to do or undergo what is unpleasant or burdensome or painful, and that being depressed or in poor spirits or feeling low is also inherently bad or undesirable or evil may seem obvious and uncontroversial, but the notion of *inherent* undesirability or evil runs strongly contrary to current conceptions of value. And this is not difficult to understand, for if optimum want-satisfaction over a lifetime is one and the same with a person's good, then evil for a person can only consist in some failure to achieve this optimum, such as the satisfaction of lesser wants resulting in the frustration of greater, or some sort of interference in a person's capacity for satisfying his wants (achieving his ends), or satisfying them optimally over a lifetime. This would include, e.g., deprivation of freedom or opportunity, and reduction in the capacity for action (voluntary abilities).

Thus Von Wright equates evil with a sub-class of the harmful, and the harmful with 'anything that frustrates or hampers the attainment of some end of human action' (1963: 46). Alan Gewirth (1978: 52–4) has a general division of goods: basic goods, which are the necessary preconditions of (successful) action; nonsubtractive goods, or the not losing of things one already has and which one values or prizes; and additive goods, or the obtaining of new prized things. On this account, purpose-fulfillment – one necessarily prizes all one's ends – is the sole good, and even one's not suffering the kind of evil which constitutes the lowering of the level of purpose-fulfillment (loss or deprivation of goods) is described as a 'non-subtractive' good. The word 'evil' does not even appear in the index.

Rawls too, because he conceives good for a person exclusively in terms of optimizing want-satisfactions over a lifetime (which it is the business of rationality to accomplish), has very little to say about evil. By implication it can only be the privation or diminution of goods, which include the 'primary' goods (desired by all rational persons because necessary to accomplish their ends) of liberty, opportunity, and a sense of one's own worth, as well as what each individual 'really wants' and wants most intensely. (There is no entry for 'evil' in Rawls's index either.)

The issue is simple. If a person's good is reducible to want-satisfaction or purpose-fulfillment, or a rational economy thereof, then if evil exists at all, it can only consist in some failure (frustration) or want-satisfaction or purpose-fulfillment. And since it is to be so understood, there really is no need to mention it at all. Thus, for example, there are only three references to evil in D. A. J. Richards' *A Theory of Reasons for Action*, as follows:

(1) A good physician may in fact find nothing at all satisfying in his being a physician, and thus find his being a good physician to be an evil *for him*, if it, in fact, frustrates his desires (1971: 290).
(2) One may well imagine men, whose capacities and desires are such that it would be irrational for them to decide to be moral, in the hypothetical decision situation; and, for them, if being moral would involve the substantial frustration of their desires, being a good man would be an evil (1971: 290).
(3) Similarly, the concept of the bad or the evil ... [is] explicated as equivalent to conducing to the frustration of rational desire (1971: 287n).

But neither activities nor experiences that are burdensome, unpleasant, or painful, nor the inherently undesirable subjective state of being depressed or in poor spirits can be glossed as consisting in (though the latter may be caused by) a failure of want-satisfaction or purpose-fulfillment. These things are evil (undesirable) *in themselves*. The view of the good, then, which is common to Von Wright, Gewirth, Rawls, and many others, including Richards, is quite unable to account for such obvious and important evils as burdensome labour, unpleasantness of all kinds, pain, suffering, depression, and misery.

One way out for want-satisfaction or purpose-fulfillment theorists of the good suggests itself. Depression and misery, the painful and the unpleasant, are things which everyone seeks to *avoid*. Thus to avoid one of these things constitutes a kind of want-satisfaction or purpose-fulfillment, and failure to avoid one of them constitutes a kind of want- or purpose-frustration. This has an artificiality and a *prima facie* implausibility about it, but Von Wright, at least, seems to grasp at it nevertheless. He realizes that there is a problem, for him, in connection with the evil of pain. Thus:

One basic form of ... harm is *pain* or pain-like sensations such as discomfort, ache, nausea. ... Wherein does the evil of pain lie? ... Pain is evil, I would say, only to the extent that it is disliked or shunned or unwanted (1963: 57).

Of course to be consistent, Von Wright would have to argue that pain, as evil, is a kind of harm, and as such something that frustrates the attainment of some end. And the end here could only be the avoidance of the pain!

This is strained and implausible because it invites us to suppose that avoiding an evil, such as pain, is a kind of purpose-fulfillment or want-satisfaction, and hence it is just a species of achieving or obtaining a good. But the good here is plainly nothing positive at all. According to the theory, an evil (insofar as evil needs to be mentioned at all) is the absence or privation, or the cause of the absence or privation, of a good (glossed as the satisfaction of some want or the fulfillment of some purpose). The evil of pain is a kind of privation of good, we are now invited to suppose, because the absence of pain is a kind of good. Pain is here the absence of the absence of pain, the absence of pain being something which is wanted or sought by everybody!

There is no need to underscore the artificiality. This is plainly an attempt to salvage a theory of whatever cost. It is obviously the pain that is the positive feature here, and the absence of it is the absence of an evil and not a positive good. It is fault enough in Gewirth's theory that it invites us to consider the non-deprivation of good as a kind of good rather than the deprivation of good as an evil, which is more direct, but there is no room for the evils of pain, sorrow, suffering, depression, etc., in Gewirth's scheme at all. Nor indeed can there be in any theory which construes good exclusively in terms of want-satisfactions or purpose-fulfillment since, on such a theory, evil can only consist in the failure to achieve one's desired ends. And an *absence* (which is nothing positive in itself) cannot be treated as a desired end, in the relevant sense, without absurdity, as has just been shown. It is absurd, furthermore, to treat pain, suffering, and misery, the existence of which is the source of the problem of evil and the need for theodicy, as a case of failure to satisfy one's wants or to achieve one's goals or purposes.

One notable exception to the general tendency to avoid discussion of evil altogether, or else to mention it, *en passant*, as the frustration of desires or purposes, is to be found in Bernard Gert's *The Moral Rules* (1970). Evil is, in fact, central to Gert's account of morality and to his account of value in general.

Gert defines evil as 'the object of an irrational desire' (1970: 45–6). The initial paradigms are death and pain. It is irrational, says Gert, to desire death or pain for oneself without a reason or, as he puts it, no rational man (in so far as he is rational) desires death or pain for himself without a reason. Furthermore, there is a rational consensus on this point. To seek one's own death or suffering, without a reason, i.e. not in order to prevent another evil or to create a benefit for oneself or for someone else, *just is* irrational. And this is not something that can be rationally disputed. A desire for one's own death or suffering, *per se*, simply *is* an irrational desire that can only be made rational if it is desired in order to achieve some further end (prevention of an evil or creation of a benefit for oneself or someone else).

Note that Gert is here on the side of the angels. According to Rawls and others, a desire can only be irrational if it is not in accord with a 'rational life plan', i.e. unless it frustrates the satisfaction of some other more highly rated desires. There is nothing wrong *per se* (in respect of the person's good) with the satisfaction of *any* desire, no matter what its object. But Gert says that a desire or want for one's own death or suffering, without some special justification, *just is irrational in itself*. And surely he is right about this, want-satisfaction theorists to the contrary notwithstanding. He furthermore notes: 'Defining evil as the object of an irrational desire provides an objective account of evil, and yet one which is not independent of man' (1970: 46). Gert adds to his list of evils, defined as the objects of irrational desire, disability, the loss of freedom or opportunity, and the loss of pleasure. Henceforth this list is treated as complete, though what is a cause of any one of these evils is also itself an evil.

For Gert, 'object of an irrational desire' is fundamental. No further analysis is possible. There can be no explanation, in other words, of why it is irrational to desire, e.g., one's own death or misery. It is simply a fundamental fact about which there is a rational consensus (so it is claimed). But this is unsatisfactory. I have argued that a grounding reason exists for a person, i.e. a reason bearing on the question of what the person should do, if there is something of value or worth to be achieved by the course of action in question. It is true that I said little *per se* in chapters 3 and 4 about evil or negative value, but I did say that something of value or worth is achieved if an evil is avoided, lessened, or removed. Similarly one has a reason not to do something if doing it will result in some evil coming about, being increased, or being strengthened. It is irrational to fail to act in order to achieve something of value or worth when there is no reason to the contrary, and it is irrational to do something if one knows or has good grounds for believing that some evil will result without any compensating benefit. But the good, or the evil, as the case may be, explains the irrationality, not *vice versa*. Why is it irrational to seek one's own death or misery without any compensating benefit to oneself or to anyone else? Because death and misery are *evils*. It is no good to say that they are evils because of or in respect of their being objects of irrational desires. For it is the irrationality of the desire that stands in need of explanation. One cannot say that it just *is* irrational.

Why, then, are death and pain evils, with the consequence that it is irrational to seek them without a reason? Of course it is no good saying that people do not want, or normally do not want to die or to suffer, or that they want very strongly, or normally want very strongly not to suffer or to die (to go on living and to be free of pain and misery). For wanting, as has long since been decided, cannot confer value; neither can wanting-not (wanting to avoid) confer negative value. In respect of pain, suffering, misery, anguish, depression (the contraries or opposites of pleasure and of feeling good), my answer is that just as pleasure and feeling good are *evidently* good, because they are experienced as such (because they are such in their natures), so their opposites are *evidently* bad or evil because they are experienced as such (because they are such in their natures). One no more needs an argument to establish that suffering and misery are bad than one needs an argument to establish that pleasure and a happy state of consciousness are good. That is their nature, as we who have experienced them know or, for that matter, even if we have not experienced them, for pleasure and a sense of well-being *are* qualities (pleasures) or states (sense of well-being) experienced as good, and unpleasantness and misery are qualities (unpleasantness) or states (misery) experienced as evil or bad. In other words, good or evil belong to their essential nature as felt qualities or states: if a thing is not experienced as good it is not pleasure or feeling good, and if a thing is not experienced as bad or evil, it is not unpleasantness or misery.

The explanation of why death is an evil is not so simple. Furthermore Gert does not really have his rational consensus on this (unless, of course, anyone who holds a contrary opinion thereby betrays his irrationality). Epicurus gave comfort to many (so it is said) by arguing that death was nothing to fear, pain being the only evil and dead people suffering not at all! And I have heard the same view offered by people who were quite unfamiliar with Epicurus, but were nevertheless both rational and sincere. It is fairly plain, I think, that death can be understood as an evil only if it is understood to mean *extinction*, though even if there is a continuation of individual consciousness and some kind of personal existence after death, we nevertheless cease to exist as individual human beings in the world, and that, Heaven knows, is terrifying enough. Ceasing to be is what most of us, with or without reason, fear more than anything. Of course this implies nothing more than a desire to go on living (to continue to be) and that, of course (as has just been said) is not enough to establish its value. It must be the case that one's own individual life is valuable in itself, that it is good simply to *be*. And by this we need not mean mere survival, least of all in a comatose state. The value is the value of being a conscious and active being – a subject of experience and an agent; in other words a functioning human being. (This does not imply the full range of human voluntary abilities; even a person paralysed from the neck down can be *mentally* active.) Of course it might be better to die than to suffer unbearable miseries, but this is perfectly compatible with life being good and death being evil. For one can rationally choose one evil in order to avoid another that is greater.

One might try to argue that survival as a conscious and active being was a necessary condition of the achievement of any further goods, but there is something queer about supposing life to be valuable only as a means – life itself (or existence) not being important, but only the joys and accomplishments of life, life being merely the *sine qua non* of these. Surely the joys and (seeming) accomplishments count for nothing if the life – if existence itself – does not; if it is all meaningless, pointless, empty, absurd.[1] While it is not *evident* that (continued) existence as a conscious, active being is a good (we cannot say *for* the person since otherwise, *ex hypothesi*, he/she does not exist) in the same way that it is evident that pleasure and a happy state of consciousness are goods for a conscious and active being who does exist, nevertheless to suppose the contrary – that conscious, active life has no inherent value or worth *per se* – is to take a strange and dark view indeed, and one, so far as I can see, that cannot be rationally supported. It is therefore at least not irrational to believe the contrary: life (existence) is a good, and to cease to be is an evil – under normal circumstances (when all is not hopeless) the greatest evil of all.

The other evils are disability (loss of voluntary abilities, as, e.g., through injury), loss of freedom, deprivation of opportunity,[2] and loss of pleasure. We are reminded at once of Gewirth's basic and non-subtractive goods and, in respect of freedom and opportunity, Rawls' primary goods. Rawls has nothing to say about disability (injury) or loss of pleasure. Gewirth is able to get both of them in, but under the heading of 'non-subtractive' goods. However this, as I suggested earlier, is nothing but a cover word for 'absence of evil' where the evil is some kind of deprivation (unlike pain, sorrow, suffering, or misery, though these may have a deprivation as their *cause*).

Disability, lack of opportunity, lack of freedom, constitute a lack of the conditions that make it possible to engage in successful purposeful behaviour, to formulate intentions and carry them out with some desired end in view. No one can function as an agent without freedom, opportunity, and voluntary abilities. Of course to the extent that one is deprived of these things one is deprived of the ability to accomplish one's ends and, *a fortiori*, of the ability to achieve what genuinely *is* good. The enabling conditions of

[1] The difficult question of value and meaning is taken up in detail in the concluding chapter.
[2] Gert treats loss (or deprivation) of freedom *or* opportunity as a *single* evil, but that is partly in the interest of making his moral rules a decalogue (1970: 83).

successful action, therefore, are genuinely basic or fundamental goods in the sense that they are the necessary conditions of the achievement of any other goods achievable by action. To deprive a person of them, therefore, or to reduce or lower them, is clearly an evil and *therefore* something that it is irrational to desire or seek for oneself without a reason.

Loss or deprivation of pleasure is in a class by itself. Gert cannot, of course, mean pleasure in the Benthamite sense, of a feeling created in various quantities with various degrees of purity, intensity, etc., though this is not so inaccurate as a description of the upper end of the feeling good/feeling bad continuum as it is of enjoyment. It is the loss or deprivation of the latter – things (activities, experiences, objects) that we like or find agreeable, pleasant, or fun, that we enjoy doing or having – that Gert must surely have in mind. And, of course, though different people take pleasure or delight in different things, pleasure is *per se*, a common good. So here, then, is another instance of deprivation of a common good. It is as *such* that it is (a common) evil, hence irrational to desire or seek for oneself without a reason.

As well as a general and objective account of evil, Gert has a general and objective account of good. Sometimes, he says, 'good' is used simply to mean the object of desire, or liking, or preference (notice here again the amalgamation of wanting, valuing, and finding good), but a general and objective good is something that no rational man will avoid without a reason (that it would be irrational to avoid without a reason). This will include, e.g., freedom, because to avoid freedom without a reason would be to seek to deprive oneself of (an available) freedom, which would be to seek an evil, i.e. something which it is irrational to desire or seek without a reason. Also included, *pari passu*, will be ability, opportunity, and pleasure, plus anything that is the cause of these. So, Gert claims, evil is the fundamental notion, and good (understood objectively) is defined in terms of it.

But unfortunately this juggling act (or sleight of hand) is not going to work. I have already argued that irrationality cannot, as Gert wants it to be, be taken as fundamental and unanalysable. We must explain (this kind of) irrationality in terms of the seeking of evil rather than *vice versa*. But evil is the *positive* notion only in the case of pain (which we may understand to include what is unpleasant, disagreeable, and painful, in various degrees, plus sadness, depression, and misery). For death can be made out to be an evil only on the basis of the positive value of life, and the others (disability, loss of freedom or opportunity, loss of pleasure) are clearly losses or deprivations of *goods*. The evil is explained in terms of the loss or deprivation of the good; we do not understand seeking the good – as Gert would have us do – as the avoidance of an evil, except in the case of avoiding pain.

Notice this does not mean that we can simply treat evil as the absence or privation of good. To begin with there are pain, unpleasantness, suffering, and misery, which are clearly positive evils and which must be recognized as such. But also not every absence or lack of a good is an evil. Thus Von Wright:

From our definitions of the beneficial and the harmful it does *not* follow that, if not-X is harmful, then X is beneficial, and *vice versa*. If, however, not-X is harmful, then X will be called *needed*. The needed is that, the lack or loss of which is a bad thing, an evil. The needed and the harmful are opposed as contradictories, *in the sense that* the contradictory of the needed is the harmful, and *vice versa*. The beneficial and the harmful are opposed as contraries (1963: 108).

Let us ignore Von Wright's analysis of 'harmful' as 'anything that frustrates or hampers the attainment of some end of human action', since the theory that the good consists in purpose-fulfillment is not essential to what is being said here. There are certain things, e.g. voluntary abilities, freedom, opportunity (these are Gewirth's 'basic goods'), without which no end, hence no good achievable by action, can be achieved. Therefore for anyone not to have, or to have lessened or reduced, any of these things is for that person an evil, in the sense that it prevents, hampers, or hinders successful agency, the achievement of the good, the worthwhile, or the desirable (whatever account we give of the desirable or worthwhile) by purposive action. This clearly is a kind of evil which can be understood as the deprivation of good, though it is none the less genuinely and properly called an evil for all that. But there are such things as unneeded benefits, and not to have (hence to withhold) these is no evil, either inherent or in respect of preventing (etc.) successful agency, or in any other sense, to those who do not have them or from whom they are withheld. The absence of an unneeded benefit is not in itself an evil. Yet it *is* the privation (the not having of) a good. Therefore evils other than pain cannot be identified simply with the absence or privation of a good.

What, then, of pleasure? The mere absence of some delightful object, some toy, some enjoyable activity or experience is not in itself an evil. This follows from what has just been said. Gert speaks, when first giving his list of evils (1970: 45), of the *loss* of freedom or opportunity, and also the *loss* of pleasure, and when he later compiles his set of moral rules, the first five of which are injunctions not to cause each of the five evils, he speaks of the *deprivation* of freedom or opportunity and of the *deprivation* of pleasure. Thus Rule 4 is either 'Don't cause loss of freedom or opportunity' or 'Don't deprive of freedom or opportunity' and Rule 5 is either 'Don't cause loss of pleasure' or 'Don't deprive of pleasure' (Gert 1970: 86–7). Now there is, of course, a difference between the mere absence of something and its loss. But it is not just the *loss* of voluntary abilities, freedom, and opportunity, or even their diminution that is an evil; rather their simple *absence* or their insufficiency is an evil for the person who suffers them, whether they ever had them or not. A person who is born blind or paralysed from the waist down is as badly off as someone who loses his sight or the voluntary control of his lower limbs. It is *as bad* one way or the other; in either case the abilities (to see, to walk) are not present.

By contrast, if I do not have some pleasurable experience, it cannot be said that this constitutes an evil for me, unless it was an experience which I had been expecting or counting on and of which I was deprived, which is the genuine suffering of a loss. I do not need to *lose* my freedom or my voluntary abilities for their absence to be an evil for me, but I actually need to have what is pleasant or enjoyable taken from my grasp, as it were, before it can be said to be an evil. So, whereas it is only the *loss* of a pleasure that is an evil, and not its mere absence, it is the simple absence of ability or freedom or opportunity or their presence in an inadequate degree that is evil, as well as their loss. Of course Gert's chief concern is to derive and justify his moral rules, and his way of putting it fits his scheme. (Evil = loss of freedom or opportunity; corresponding rule = 'Don't cause loss of freedom or opportunity'. Evil = loss of pleasure; corresponding rule = 'Don't cause loss of pleasure'.) But it is only necessary that the *absence*, not the loss of a thing be an evil, in order for *causing* its loss to be the bringing of an evil upon a person. So Gert might as well have said *absence* of ability, freedom, and opportunity. But it is not the mere absence of something *pleasant or enjoyed* that is an evil, but its actual loss. The word 'deprivation' is no help here, since it can mean (and does mean in the formulation of Gert's rules) the actual *taking away* of something, or its mere absence (as when we say that someone is culturally deprived). It is only in the first sense that the deprivation of pleasure is an evil. Of course the deprivation of pleasure *in general* would be an evil, since some pleasure in life is *needed*. But that is not what Gert means.

We are left, then, with the following picture. There is at least one class of evils that cannot be explained at all in terms of the absence, loss, withholding, or removal of good (whether or not that is glossed in terms of desire-satisfaction or purpose-fulfillment), namely those that are the contrary or opposite of (a) pleasure, and (b) feeling good, including the unpleasant, the disagreeable, the painful, the agonizing; suffering, sorrow, misery, and despair. These are inherent positive evils and not the mere privation of good.

Secondly, there are the evils which are constituted by the absence, or presence in insufficient degree of the universal and necessary conditions of successful agency (Gewirth's basic goods, Gert's third and fourth evils), namely voluntary ability (the evil of disablement), freedom, and opportunity (the evils of lack of freedom and lack of opportunity). These evils result from the absence, or presence in insufficient degrees, of a certain class of common goods (the necessary conditions of successful agency), goods because they are necessary conditions of the achievement of any good achievable by action. (If we were to add income and self-respect, for which, perhaps, some sort of a case could be made out, then we would have Rawls' primary goods.) Their absence *is* an evil and it is mere obfuscation to say, as Gewirth does (in order to do value theory entirely in terms of goods without mention of evil), that the absence of this absence is a good, and to claim that *that* is what we are really talking about.

Thirdly there is the evil which consists in the actual removal, by whatever agency, of someone's present or anticipated enjoyable activity, experience, or object of delight. It is an evil to suffer such a loss. Nor is it enlightening to describe this sort of evil as the absence of a 'non-subtractive good'.

No theory of value is adequate, then, if it does not give an account of evil as well as of good. Nor is it sufficient simply to recognize those evils which hinder or prevent successful agency and thereby the achievement of particular goods. For, in addition to these, there are, first of all, suffering and misery, which are the commonest and most obvious of evils, and which, being positive in themselves, cannot be so glossed. And there is the loss of present and expected pleasure, which is not a mere privation of good (*that* is not, as such, evil), but the taking away of a good that one already has in one's grasp. To this list we might add, if excellence or virtue is a personal good in the quasi-Platonic way I suggested in chapter 6, the loss or diminution of an excellence or virtue as an inherent personal evil.

Gert's attempt to treat evil as fundamental, and to define good in terms of it, goes too far in the opposite direction. There is a sense in which the opposites of pleasure and of feeling good (being in good spirits), i.e. what is disagreeable or painful and the state of feeling miserable, are the only positive evils, for the evil nature of all the other evils, although they are genuine evils and must be recognized as such, is to be understood in terms of either preventing, hindering, or hampering successful agency and hence the achievement of good, or the taking away or removal of some good which is already in a person's grasp.

On the very first page I said that the goods achievable by action, to which reasons for and against (grounding reasons) are related, included evils reducible, eliminable, or avoidable. And throughout I have glossed 'good' or 'valuable' or 'desirable', treated as synonyms, as 'what is worth having, getting, or doing'. I might have added, although I did not, that the reduction, elimination, or avoidance of an evil is something worth having, getting, or doing. One can, in other words, for general theoretical purposes, treat the reduction, elimination, or avoidance of evil as a kind of good, valuable, or desirable end. And there is no harm in this, for it does not commit one to the view (now shown to be false) that evil is nothing but the absence or deprivation of good. In fact, rather the opposite, for if evil were nothing but the absence or diminution or deprivation of good, then preventing, reducing, or eliminating evil would, as the prevention, reduction, or elimination of the absence, diminution, or deprivation of good, be logically and hence extensionally equivalent to the increasing, bringing about, or preservation of a positive good, the view we have just found wanting. And there would be, if this equivalence held, no *point* in any reference to the prevention, reduction, or elimination of evil. The prevention, reduction, or elimination of evil, then, though distinct from the achievement of positive good, can be seen as a species of good or value to be sought, and hence as providing grounding reasons for action, and the theoretical structure of the first five chapters remains intact.

However we must not let the adequacy of this simple theoretical structure lull us into supposing that the prevention, reduction, or elimination of evil is *on all fours with* the production, increase, or conservation of good, as if the one could for all practical purposes be treated as an instance of the other or *vice versa* (good = negative evil; evil = negative good). Good and evil remain significantly different, even if some evils do consist in the deprivation of good or of the means to its achievement, and some goods, e.g. the so-called 'basic' goods can be regarded as the absence of evil. (These are also what Von Wright calls *needs*.) For it is far worse to suffer an evil, of whatever kind, than to fail to have or acquire some unneeded benefit. And this is of the profoundest importance for our understanding of morality.

I have dealt throughout this chapter with *personal* evil, i.e. what is evil for the person on whom it falls. *Moral* evil, I suggest, is to be understood in terms of acting in ways that cause or tend to cause evil to fall on others. Still, if moral virtue, as a kind of virtue or excellence, is a species of personal good, as I tried to argue in the last chapter, then its opposite, moral vice, is perhaps also a personal evil, even if not, as Plato thought, the greatest personal evil. But whether that is true or not, the evil man is *socially* evil (a cause of evil to his fellows) and is to be shunned, perhaps punished, for the evil he causes. But these moral topics must be left for another time.

8

Meaning, value, and practical judgments

What gives life significance or meaning? Why does anything matter? Given that all individual lives end in death, and given the general impermanence of things (everything most ultimately perish), do any of our activities or any of our projects have any point? Does anything ultimately really matter at all? (All is vanity, saith the preacher.) But if, in the end, nothing matters at all, since all comes to nothing, nothing is really valuable or worthwhile; there is no such thing as value in the world. Contrariwise, if there is such a thing as value in the world, value achievable by action, then some things are worth doing (having, getting) and, so it would seem, life is worth living and does have significance or meaning.

This internal relation between the possibility of its being true that something is valuable or worthwhile (the possibility of a thing's *being* worthwhile, as opposed to being merely desired, or only thought worthwhile) and one's actions, hence one's life having meaning or significance is pointed to and developed by David Wiggins in his 1976 British Academy Lecture. He suggests there that this question of meaning and the related question of whether anything can *be* worthwhile (or, as he prefers it, whether a statement that something is worthwhile can be true) are the central questions of ethics (1976: 331–2). The place of meaning, he says, has been usurped by happiness (glossed either as desire-satisfaction, or pleasure and the absence of pain), and the question of whether practical judgments (to the effect that something ought to be done) can be true, has been usurped by the problem of answering the question, 'What shall I do?'

I would myself say that these questions (all four of them) belonged to axiology, or (somewhat more narrowly) to practical philosophy in general, rather than to ethics, whose subject matter is restricted to moral value, and I do not regard this as simply a verbal quibble. (I would not, for example, regard the present work as a study in *ethics*.) But as to the centrality of the questions, as well as their interrelation, there is no doubt whatever, though the matter seems to be not quite so simple as Wiggins believes.

I have myself argued (chapter 6) that if hedonism (although it is preferable both to non-cognitivism and to desire-satisfaction theories) were true, life would seem to lack meaning or significance, that it would amount to little in the end, and that excellence is to be sought or pursued before pleasure. When I began to read Wiggins's lecture, I thought I had encountered on ally but, by the time I had finished, I found his position so undermined by confusions and so weakened by the uncritical acceptance of some current orthodoxies, e.g. the alleged internal relation of value to desire, and the identification of ought-judgments with expressions of decisions (thus rendering them incapable of being true or false), that his championship of objective value and his assault on hedonism seemed to amount, in the end, to little more than a *cri de coeur*.

As a way of making clear my own position on these matters, I shall root out and lay bare these confusions, errors, and wrong turns in this concluding chapter.

Wiggins wishes to attack the view that psychological states are the source of all value, insisting that value, or some aspects of it, are to be found *in the world as object* not in the psychological states of the person for whom a thing has value. Value, in other words, is a matter not, or not exclusively of desideration, of commitment of the will, of pleasure (construed as an inherently valuable subjective state), or satisfactions (in our second sense). Thus he has to take on a great many views which, unfortunately, he is not always careful to distinguish clearly, for much of the time treating them all indiscriminately as a composite, labelled 'non-cognitivism'.

The views include (1) that of Richard Taylor (his chief stalking-horse), as expressed in his *Good and Evil* (1970), where he argues that what alone gives worth or value to an activity is that it is desired, (2) the meta-ethical non-cognitivism of those, such as R. M. Hare (1952), who hold that there is no value prior to commitment of some kind, (3) existentialists such as Sartre, whose views are remarkably similar, (4) classical utilitarians, such as Bentham and Mill, interpreted as claiming that happiness (glossed as pleasure and the absence of pain) as the one inherently desirable subjective state, is the sole good, and (5) contemporary 'neutral' utilitarians, who see the end of action as maximizing or (through a rational economy) optimizing want or desire-satisfaction, whatever the wants or desires are for. What all these views have in common is the belief that the source of value is *within*, and is not to be found in the world outside. For the locus of value, you must look to the inner world of the agent as it is for him (or her). Or, as one might otherwise put it, value is in some sense purely subjective, whether it is a creation or invention or projection of the valuer (Hare, Sartre, Mackie), a product of an agent's desire or will (R. Taylor) or whether it reposes in inherently desirable subjective states (hedonistic or neutral utilitarianism). The opposing view is that it is there, or partly there, to be discovered in the world outside the wanter or valuer's subjective states.

Wiggins' composite non-cognitivist is construed as holding that the assertibility conditions of value-judgments are not truth conditions (that the assertibility condition of value judgments falls short of truth) and, of course this is a way of expressing the meta-ethical (or meta-axiological) non-cognitivists' view. But it does not apply to Taylor, who would not touch meta-ethics with a barge-pole, nor to utilitarians of whatever variety.[1] Taylor's non-cognitivism, perhaps better called anti-cognitivism (he himself calls it 'anti-rationalism'), does not deny, even implicitly, that value-judgments can be *true*. Indeed, on Taylor's view, it is a sufficient condition of something's being good or desirable or worthwhile for *A*, that *A* desires to do (have, get) it. And that is a straightforward factual matter. What Taylor denies is that value is a matter of objective or rational cognition or discovery as is claimed, e.g. by Plato or Kant. Rather value lies entirely in desire. *Wanting* (inclinational) to do a thing alone makes it worthwhile; but it really *does* make it worthwhile; if I want to do something it is *true* that it is worth my while. Benthamist utilitarianism too is, as meta-axiology, a cognitivist doctrine, ascribing value solely to the subjective state of pleasure or the subjective state of being satisfied. Whether or not someone is enjoying himself or is satisfied is again a straightforward factual matter. So, at least with respect to Taylor's theory and to either form of utilitarianism, Wiggins' enquiry into the assertibility condition(s) of evaluative and practical judgments is an *ignoratio elenchi*.

Wiggins wants to establish that value is a matter involving features of the world beyond the merely subjective, but he confuses

[1] R. M. Hare possibly excepted. (See Hare 1972).

this with the narrower question of whether value judgments in general, or practical judgments in particular, can be true. They could, of course, be true (as has just been shown) while the locus of value remained exclusively in subjective states. Wiggins is plainly of the opinion that one's actions, hence one's life, cannot be meaningful or worthwhile, unless they are directed to some purpose or goal beyond mere subjective satisfaction. But if this were so, then the possibility of the truth of value-judgments would not, contrary to what he claims, be a sufficient condition of our lives being meaningful or worthwhile.

Wiggins' chief objection to the view that value lies exclusively in subjective states is expressed as follows:

... No attempt to make sense of the human condition can make sense of it if it treats the objects of psychological states as unequal partners or derivative elements in the conceptual structure of values and states and their objects (1976: 348).

What is valuable, in other words, is not just the psychological state, understood as such, i.e. as a bit of subjectivity – pleasure, good feeling or whatever – but includes, from the agent's perspective, the object of that state; for what is of value is, for the agent, phenomenally objective – something that impinges on him or her from outside. The 'non-cognitivist' invites us to see value from the perspective of the person for whom it is a value, but seems to ignore what it is actually *like* from that perspective. As it might otherwise be put, though Wiggins does not put it this way, the account given by the 'non-cognitivist' (the composite discussed above) is phenomenologically inadequate.

Of the phenomenal objectivity of value, Wiggins gives the following example:

A man comes at dead of night to a hotel in a place where he has never been before. In the morning he stumbles out from his darkened room and, following the scent of coffee out of doors, he finds a sunlit terrace looking out across a valley on to a range of blue mounains in the half-distance. The sight of them – a veritable vale of Tempe – entrances him. In marvelling at the valley and mountains he thinks only how overwhelmingly beautiful they are. *The value of the state depends on the value attributed to the object.* But the theory which I oppose says all non-instrumental value resides here in the man's own state, and in the like states of others who are actually so affected by the mountains ... What I am saying about the theory is simply that it is untrue to the actual experience of the object-directed states which are the starting-point of that theory (1976: 347n).

More abstractly, he puts it as follows:

The participant, with the going concepts of the objective and the worthwhile, descries certain external properties in things and states of affairs. And the presence there of these properties is what invests them with importance in his eyes. The one thing the properties cannot be, at least for him, is mere projections resulting from a certain kind of efficacy in the causation of satisfaction. For no appetitive or aesthetic or contemplative state can see its own object as having a value which is derivative in the way which is required by the thesis that all non-instrumental value resides in human states of satisfaction (1976: 347).

This is supposed to apply not only to aesthetic and contemplative, but to all 'appetitive' states as well. The very persuasive example, however (given in the first extract quoted above), is aesthetic. And the perception of beauty and other desirable aesthetic qualities is surely here the paradigm. In chapter 4 (pp. 63–4) I referred to this as the further objectivity that the value of a thing may possess beyond its simply being the object of a personal like or dislike, an objectivity which must exist if there is to be aesthetic appreciation beyond mere likes and dislikes. If it is, however, a *simple* hedonic matter, then no such *further* objectivity need be involved, although, of course, value dependent upon personal taste is perfectly objective in the primary sense that it requires *discovery*, and is in no way dependent upon desire or the will.

What, then, of *appetitive* states? My suspicion here is that what Wiggins really means is *hedonic* states, and that he is confusing (as so many philosophers regularly do) the desire for a thing (motivational propensity) with the *enjoyment* of it. But, as I have been at pains to argue, the former belongs in the realm of motivation exclusively, and only the latter belongs in the realm of value. That this confusion is at work here is confirmed when Wiggins says that to ignore the object of psychological states is 'far worse than Aristotle's opposite error' of claiming that we desire an object because it seems good to us. We are, he says, to treat psychological states and their objects as equal and reciprocal partners', but the psychological state he goes on to talk about is the state of *desire*, and he proceeds to talk about the reciprocity of desire and the (seeming) good. However, the relevant psychological state here is not desire (unless the reference is all the way back to Taylor) but *satisfaction*(s) (human states of satisfaction). (This is perhaps another of the bad consequences of lumping

Taylor, Hare, Mill, *et al.* together as a composite stalking horse; although perhaps one could argue with equal force that the general tendency to lump together desire, what is thought to have worth, and actual value, may have been a factor influencing the original lumping.)

For in the present example the psychological state and its object that are to be seen as equal and reciprocal partners can only be the delight at beholding the beauty of the valley and the mountains and that beauty itself as a perceived quality of the scene. Actually desire is here *completely* irrelevant, since the person in the example comes upon the scene quite unexpectedly, without any pre-existing appetite, inclination, or reflective desire for the object in question or for an object of that kind. He was not *setting out* to have an experience of beauty. In fact this is just the kind of example that can standardly be used to show that the experience of value need not be dependent upon the existence of desires of any kind. 'Desiring,' says Wiggins, ' . . . is one part of what is required for there to be such a thing as the perspective for which the noninstrumental goodness of x is there to be perceived (1976: 348).' But no desire exists in the present case at all! What we have to say about this and other desirable aesthetic experiences is, I think, that an object as experienced is perceived as possessing aesthetic value or worth (the value could be beauty) and one's joy or delight (hedonic value) is in response to this perception.

Nor is there any question of desire and its objects being in some sort of 'made for each other' balance or equilibrium in the simple hedonic case, since desire is equally irrelevant there. Rather it would have to be some sort of equilibrium between pleasure or enjoyment and the object enjoyed; it would have to be that the object of pleasure was made for enjoyment and *vice versa*. Now it is conceivable that this is true, in some sense, but it is not really relevant to the question of the objectivity of value, or of whether value judgments can be true. That the thing is liked, together with the fact that this is in no way dependent upon desire or the will, is enough to establish that. And as to the *further* kind of objectivity, which Wiggins wants to attribute, it does *not* have that, since liking or preference is often a personal matter (different people like or prefer different things).

Also, in the aesthetic case, the beauty or other desirable aesthetic quality is perceived as lying in the aesthetic object as it is perceived, and the aesthetic joy or delight is in response to the perception of these phenomenally objective qualities, qualities that are seen as coming to us or impinging on us from outside. But in the *simple* hedonic case, as for example when I am enjoying my game of golf I am engaging in some activity in the world that has a certain character I find to be pleasant or agreeable. But the value lies in my finding it pleasant or agreeable; unlike the aesthetic case, there is no *value* that is phenomenally objective, but only a quality that is agreeable *as experienced*. Of course the world beyond my subjectivity is involved because I am engaged in a social activity, and it is not that these things are instrumentally valuable as the cause of my pleasure (regarded as an inherently desirable subjective state). That is a completely false picture; it is enjoyed *for its own sake* and its value is in its being personally agreeable.

The case of an agreeable *sensation* is somewhat different, for while the sensation may have an external cause, it is not the cause which is enjoyed. What is enjoyed is the feeling, and feelings are subjective. (Nevertheless even this kind of value remains objective in my primary sense, since the fact that I enjoy a certain feeling or sensation is something that must be discovered and is not dependent upon desire or the will.) And even this is to be contrasted with *pure good feeling* (pp. 103–4 above), or being in good spirits which, even when there is an intentional object (feeling good *about* something), is an independent and self-contained hedonic state, since that object is also the (mental) cause of the feeling (the 'high'). This genuinely *is* a case of an inherently desirable or valuable subjective state existing in and of itself and not having its being in, e.g. an activity or an object of experience or even a sensation. Wiggins' implicit claim that it is always false to the internal (intentional) point of view that value lies in subjective states cannot be made. Nevertheless the statement that such a state is inherently valuable is objectively true; its assertibility condition does not fall short of regular truth!

Here we come back to Wiggins' original claim that the question of whether one's action, hence one's life had a meaning, depended upon whether value-assertions were ever true, as if the latter (it being always understood that there is a subjective element) were a sufficient condition of the former. But what Wiggins is really claiming is that our actions and our lives cannot be said to have meaning or importance or significance unless value consists in something more than mere pleasure or satisfaction; if hedonism were true, then life would be lacking in meaning and significance. And this is very much in accord with what I argued in Chapter 6. Of course the belief that life is worth living and that it has meaning or significance depends upon the belief that some things are valuable or worthwhile, and it follows that this possibility is a *necessary* condition of life's being meaningful or significant. Yet something more than this is needed.

Wiggins believes that if the possibility of truth for some value-assertions bearing on what we should do (values achievable by action) could be established, then we would have established a kind of objectivity for value, namely its existing beyond mere subjective states, that would settle the case. But the possibility of the truth of value-assertions does not establish objectivity of this kind. For that some value-assertions are true is perfectly compatible, for instance, with the brand of hedonism that would locate value exclusively in inherently desirable or undesirable subjective states. In order to show that value exists *in objects*, some further argument is necessary. Nor is it even clear that if we could establish that there was objective value in this sense, we would *ipso facto* have shown that life was indeed meaningful.

Let us try and sort this out. As has been said, that some things (ends) are genuinely worthwhile is a necessary condition of our actions, hence our lives, having meaning or significance. This in itself is enough to take care of the genuine non-cognitivists. For the genuine non-cognitivist denies that there is such a thing as value, value being equivalent to valuing, and that, in turn, being equivalent to wanting or desiring. For the non-cognitivist there is nothing but wanting or desiring. There is no real good. And since the condition of the existence of genuine value is not satisfied, a necessary condition of life's possessing meaning or significance is not satisfied. So much, on this particular score, for genuine non-cognitivism.

Richard Taylor presents the matter differently. He is not a non-cognitivist and does not deny the existence of value; rather, in his view the fact that we desire to do a thing *gives* it value, or bestows value upon it. Desire is the magic source of value in what is otherwise a valueless universe. There is a world of difference here. On Taylor's theory some value-utterances related to action can be true, but none the less *value does not go beyond the subjective*. It is *true* that some things (ends, activities) are genuinely worthwhile, but it is contingent or arbitrary which things are worthwhile – namely whatever a desiderative being, whether man or beast, happens to desire. The only measure of worth is strength of desire. Cognition of value is totally absent, as is any rational reflection on the worth or importance of various ends. It is this that Wiggins is really objecting to, and it is an objection with which I am in complete sympathy.

Let us now consider utilitarianism as a theory of value, first the hedonistic, then the 'neutral' (want-satisfaction) variety. The hedonistic form of utilitarianism can take one of two forms or can combine the two. The first kind would be the view that the only truly desirable end is to feel as good as possible for as long a time as possible. This would place feeling good or 'high' (being in good spirits) in the position of the only good, and feeling bad (being depressed or in poor spirits) in the position of the only evil. And, as has been said, feeling good is an inherently desirable, feeling bad an inherently undesirable, subjective state. Both may have various causes, but both may be, e.g., drug-induced. (If we wanted a word, we might dub this 'euphorism'.) Again something, viz. euphoria, is said to be genuinely worth achieving, but again, *pace* Wiggins, this is *not* enough to make life meaningful, for again it fails to go beyond the merely subjective, and cognition is not in the picture at all.

The second form of hedonistic utilitarianism as a theory of value would hold that one should spend as much time as possible doing or undergoing what one enjoys (likes) doing or undergoing, and as little time as possible doing or undergoing what one finds unpleasant or disagreeable. Pleasant or agreeable activities and experiences assume the position of the one true good, and unpleasant or disagreeable activities and experiences that of the one true evil. Now, except in the case of agreeable or disagreeable sensations, pleasure and its opposite do normally involve cognition of, and other interrelationships with, objects in the world. Of course all that is required is the *belief* that one is interrelating with the world beyond one's subjectivity. The belief could be *false,* at least in theory (imagine a complicated machine attached to the brain) and the pleasure or unpleasantness just as keen. If one were to argue that it was rational to arrange to be deceived in this way so as to have the enjoyable experiences, this would be tantamount to saying that it is, after all, the inherently desirable subjective state that really counts. But the present kind of hedonist need not hold such a view. He could hold that the experience did not possess real value unless the relevant beliefs were true (that one is acting in the world, that one is engaging in an activity with others). But if the value nevertheless lies in the felt quality of the activity or experience, even though it is a necessary condition of its being valuable that genuine cognition is taking place, this would still not seem to be enough to satisfy Wiggins. For it is not objective value in his sense, i.e. value that lies in the world, that is being cognized, and that seems to be for him a necessary condition of one's purposes, hence one's life, having worth.

Neutral or want-satisfaction utilitarianism, as a theory of value, would plainly be more objectionable for Wiggins. (Note that a want-satisfaction theory of value does not have to be utilitarian. Rawls, Richards, and Harman hold such views, yet none of them is a utilitarian.) For the claim is made here that the satisfaction of a want *constitutes* a realized value, and the degree of the value depends upon the strength or intensity of the want. This is a view similar to Taylor's, but it is not exactly the same. Taylor argues that the wanting itself confers value on the activity wanted (on doing the thing that one wants to do). He says little or nothing about satisfactions. Satisfactions, however, are *the thing* for neutral utilitarians and other want-satisfaction theorists. Want-satisfaction is indeed the one true good for such theorists, and want-frustration the one true evil. I have objected (chapter 3, also Bond 1979) that getting what one wants is no guarantee of value-realization, nor even of satisfaction, in the hedonic sense. That an agent's *desire* is satisfied is no guarantee that the *agent* will be satisfied (feel satisfaction) or indeed gain anything. But this is not Wiggins objection. His objection is, once more, that this is nothing but a (supposedly inherently desirable) subjective state, and the kind of value that gives meaning or significance to one's actions and one's life must be a value that goes beyond mere subjectivity.

Another way of putting Wiggins' position might be the following. An action (or its end) only possesses *true* value, of the kind that makes it (or its attainment) truly worthwhile, if this is a value that goes beyond the value (if such there be) of subjective states. The value *attributed* to subjective states cannot be the genuine article. Or perhaps Wiggins believes that it is simply a mistake to believe that subjective states possess value of any kind; value *as perceived* is phenomenally objective and must therefore *be* objective (in Wiggins' full sense of existing in the world beyond mere subjective states), if it is to be real, i.e. to possess the nature it is thought to possess, which is objective. In either case, our actions and our lives only have significance or meaning or importance if there are values *out there* to be cognized and discovered and sought by the agent-observer.

The possibility of value-assertions being true may yield us only hedonic values, or values conferred by desire, or values of desire-satisfaction. If Wiggins means to deny that values of the second or third kind exist at all, I am in full agreement with him. Desire cannot confer value, and desire-satisfaction is neither a necessary nor a sufficient condition for the realization of value, as I have argued at length. (Still, Wiggins does not take this line.) Hedonic value, however, is quite genuine, whether we think of feeling good (or bad), pleasant (or painful) sensations or activities, experiences other than sensations that are enjoyed (or found disagreeable), or objects in which one takes delight (or which one finds repellent). Indeed it is difficult to see how anyone could deny that these are quite genuine values. (Part of Wiggins' difficulty in not being able to see that they are genuine values is perhaps because he does not take care to distinguish carefully enough theories which construe value in terms of desirable subjective states from the non-cognitivism towards which so much of his argument is directed.) If they *are* genuine values, why is their reality and the possibility of attaining them not enough to make life significant or meaningful? Wiggins does not and cannot provide us with the answer.

I would regard all such (hedonic) values as objective, in my primary sense, since they are not dependent upon desire or the will. Furthermore, the judgments that pleasure and feeling good are themselves values are objectively true. Such value, indeed, is actually experienced; it is neither observed nor inferred. Of course it is not objective in Wiggins' sense of being out there in the world to be cognized. But does this render it spurious? I should certainly have thought not. (It could only be thought to be spurious if it were tied, as it is by Wiggins, to non-cognitivism, or the belief that evaluative judgments are not capable of being true or false.) That Wiggins takes as paradigmatic the example of being struck by the beauty of the valley and the hills, shows that he supposes *all* value to be apprehended as phenomenally objective, as aesthetic value is.

Pleasure and feeling good are, in their natures, *experienced* as values, though pleasure is always *in* something, and feeling good is often *about* something, both of which (except in the case of pure sensations) will involve beliefs about the world beyond pure subjectivity. And that, indeed, is important. The pleasure of *simulated* activities and experiences, or delight in simulated objects, *though experientially indistinguishable from the real thing*, would not have the same kind or degree of value that pleasure in real activities, experiences, or objects has. Pleasure of this kind really does take us beyond the realm of pure subjectivity and into the world. Should Wiggins not, perhaps, be satisfied with this?

To recapitulate. Wiggins believes that the possibility of the truth of some evaluative judgments implies that there is genuine value to be gained by action, hence that life can be meaningful or significant. This possibility is denied by non-cognitivism and (Wiggins implies) by existentialism, by theories (e.g. Taylor's) according to which desire confers value, hedonistic theories, and want-satisfaction theories. However, as we have seen, it is not denied by any of the last three. We can dismiss the theories according to which desire confers value, and the want-satisfaction theories, on grounds that are not available to Wiggins, who clings to the belief that desire is somehow internally related to value. This leaves us with hedonism, and about the genuineness of hedonic value there seems to be no doubt whatever, even if we wish to deny that it is the *only* value. But hedonic value is not good enough for Wiggins, as both his abstract argument and his example (both quoted above) illustrate. He thinks it is not good enough because, at least by implication, it implies that value judgments cannot be true. But it does not imply that. Therefore, if Wiggins is to continue to reject it as insufficient to make life meaningful, he must do so on other grounds. He must acknowledge that at least a kind of value may exist, one achievable by action, which nevertheless cannot make life meaningful. Or, in other words (always assuming a subjective element), the possibility of the truth of value judgments is a necessary but not a sufficient condition of our actions and our lives being significant or meaningful. Pleasure, though a genuine value, is not enough; something more is needed. But hedonism must be rejected on grounds other than that it denies truth to value judgments.

Wiggins thinks the something more is value or value-properties as they exist in the world to be discovered or cognized by a desiderative human being. Aesthetic value is the paradigm, and possibly 'contemplative' value as well. (How Aristotelian this is!) My own proposal, as put forward in chapter 6 (also Greek-sounding) was the pursuit of excellence or virtue in general as the condition of special merit or worth, and therefore of self-respect, a necessary condition of happiness (where 'happiness' is not glossed hedonistically). Aesthetic appreciation is important in a full and complete and meaningful life, and perhaps the contemplation of being (seen as possessing value) is an important part of the most complete and meaningful life, though here we edge dangerously towards obscurantism. But the pursuit of excellence (moral virtue, development and exercise of one's talents, doing *well* things that are worth doing) is surely a necessary condition of a meaningful existence.

Wiggins draws a distinction as follows:

I propose that we distinguish between valuations (typically recorded in verdicts of the form 'x is good', 'bad', 'beautiful', 'ugly', ignoble', 'brave', 'just', 'mischievous', 'malicious', 'worthy', 'honest', 'corrupt', 'disgusting', 'amusing', 'diverting', 'boring', etc. – no restrictions at all on the category of x) and *directives* or *deliberative* (or *practical*) judgments (e.g. 'I must ψ,' 'I ought to ψ', 'it would be best, all things considered, for me to ψ', etc).... That there is much in between pure valuations and pure directives ... does nothing to obstruct the discrimination I seek to effect between the spurious fact–value distinction and the real is–ought distinction (1976: 338).

To the list of valuations are added 'dishonest' and 'priggish' (1976: 359). Wiggins holds that, so far as *valuations* are concerned, non-cognitivism, or the claim that the assertibility condition of value judgments falls short of truth, has nothing in its favour, that is unless we were to exclude all non-primary qualities (e.g. 'red', 'chair', 'earthquake', 'person', 'famine') as well (1976: 363). If Peircean convergence for all possible rational beings is the condition of factuality, then factuality is very narrow indeed. But while the fact–value distinction is spurious, the is–ought distinction is genuine, according to Wiggins. Whereas evaluations are objective in any relevant sense, directive or deliberative judgments would be thoroughly objective only if there were a practical rationality for all conceivable rational agents. Something of non-cognitivism must be preserved, he thinks, where practical judgments – judgments as to what one should do or not do – are concerned. To make use of Wiggins' own contrast between invention and discovery: where valuations are concerned, all is discovery; it is a mistake to suppose that it is a matter of invention. (That, supposedly, is what is wrong with the complex of rejected theories of value.) But an element of invention does come in where deliberative or practical judgments ('directives') are concerned. Here, and only here, a remnant of non-cognitivism is to be saved.

Or that is what Wiggins's doctrine *sometimes* looks like, especially if we attend to the passage just quoted. But later in his address Wiggins argues that there is a doctrine to be reconstructed 'from the assets of bankrupted or naive non-cognitivism' (1976: 366) which he calls the doctrine of 'cognitive underdetermination'. Whereas naive non-cognitivism contradicts itself by directing us to the internal viewpoint, while ignoring the (supposed) phenomenal objectivity of value from within that viewpoint, cognitive underdetermination does not. 'It is consistent with its own rationale'.

What the new position will say is that, in as much as anything matters, and in as much as human life has the meaning we think it has, that possibility is rooted in a species of invention which is none the less arbitrary, contingent, and (taken as a whole) objectively indefensible for having been gradual, unconscious and communal. Our form of life – or that in our form of life which gives individual lives meaning – is not something which as a species we strictly speaking discovered, or can regulate or adjust by reference to what is true or correct. And, even within the going enterprise of our existing concerns and deliberative judgements, it is only an illusion that the assertibility of such judgements is truth (Wiggins 1976: 365–6).

And again:

Aristotle wrote (*N. E.* 1094ª23): 'Will not knowledge of the good have a great influence on life? Shall we not, like archers who have a mark to aim at, be more likely to hit upon the right thing?' But in reality there is not such thing as *The Good* no such thing as knowledge of it, and nothing fixed independently of ourselves to aim at. Or so runs the thesis of cognitive underdetermination (1976: 367–8).

The thesis of cognitive underdetermination is understood to apply to value judgments across the board, both valuations and 'directives', and in consistency, one would expect to see Wiggins launch an attack on it, at least as regards the former. But all he does is suggest that, perhaps, objectivity could be combined with cognitive underdetermination, making use of an analogy with Wittgenstein's normative conception of mathematics (1976: 369–70). But *these* remarks apparently apply as much to practical judgments as to valuations. In *both* these areas we are to consider the compossibility of objectivity, discovery, *and* invention (1976: 371). In his summary (1976: 372), furthermore, Wiggins describes himself as having concluded that there is no 'overwhelming reason' to deny practical judgments their objectivity, whether they can be said to be true or not, and whatever the extent and importance of cognitive underdetermination is. (He does not allow that it might have *no* extent or importance.) But as to valuations ('valuational predicates') he declares himself to have concluded that it is senseless to deny that these are properties in a world, though they are not primary qualities. What is important is that they are 'objectively discriminable and can impinge upon practical appreciation and judgment' (1976: 372).

Further that human lives have point is *to some extent* dependent upon the disposition in the world of value properties. There is no question of a 'free-floating commitment' as might be suggested by an existentialist or a 'naive' non-cognitivist. Cognitive underdetermination, however, though it does not imply this 'free-floating commitment', shows that life's point 'may depend *as much* upon something invented (not necessarily *arbitrarily*), or upon something contributed by the liver of the life, as it depends upon something discovered' (1976: 373). And, he goes on: 'Or it may depend upon what the liver of the life brings to the world in order to see the world in such a way as to discover meaning.' Presumably this is not what any and every liver brings to a life, since that would result in pure (anthropocentric) objectivity, but what particular individuals or members or particular cultures bring to their lives.

It is not exactly clear where all this leaves us. How true is 'cognitive underdetermination'? Or what is its 'extent' and 'importance'? One is led to expect that it will apply only to 'directives' (practical judgments) and not to valuations. But as it is put forward it clearly applies to both. There is such a thing as 'non-cognitivist relativism' which says that 'all strict valuations [*n.b.*] . . . have the interesting property that the interpretation of the value predicate presupposes a shared viewpoint, and a set of concerns common between interpreter and subject' (1976: 364). But how is this consistent with the claim that whereas the supposed fact–value distinction does not exist, the is–ought distinction is genuine? Surely what is sauce for the goose is sauce for the gander? If valuations and 'directives' are in the same boat, so far as the extent or importance of cognitive underdetermination is concerned – a cognitive underdetermination that might nevertheless leave them objective after all – what is the basis of the distinction between practical judgments, where something more is required for an 'ought' than an 'is', and valuations, where it is claimed that value predicates describe objective properties characterizing an (anthropocentric and possibly, to a degree, ethnocentric) world?

A search for clues yields the following possible reasons for the existence of an is–ought gap, although no fact–value gap exists. (1) Practical judgments are decisions which, as such, and unlike appreciations, are not capable of being true or false (1976: 339 and 339n). (2) There is no *a priori* theory of (cosmic) rationality; therefore rationality, and with it practical judgments, must be relative to 'ideals of agency and rationality', and this is a relativity which goes beyond whatever relativity (or cognitive underdetermination) attaches to value predicates (1976: 361, 364). (3) Since they are decisions or involve decisions, practical judgments fit the world to the discourse, rather than *vice versa*; therefore it could not be the state of the world (facts) that made them true (1976: 370 and 370n). (4) Since there exist undecidable practical questions (questions about what one ought to do), the law of excluded middle is abrogated and one of the conditions of regular truth defeated (1976: 371).

The answers are as follows. (1) 'Ought', 'should', 'must', etc. judgments are not and do not mark decisions about what to do; rather they mark stages in deliberation (taking note of the reasons for and against various alternatives and their relative stringency) or the conclusion of deliberation. But after one has decided what one ought to do, all things considered, one must then decide what to do and do it, or do nothing at all. One may do, without effort of will, what one judges one ought to do, all things considered, if there are no opposing inclinations; or it may require resolution or strength of will to do it, if opposing inclinations are to be mastered; or one may say, 'To hell with it' and give in to the opposing inclinations. In all three cases one's judgment concerning what one ought to do (or to have done) remains unaltered.

(2) True, there is no 'cosmic' practical rationality. That is because

there is no practical reasoning from *no* point of view. Values must be values *for* someone (or everyone). Similarly there could be no values in a subjectless universe, or in a universe understood in terms of Galilean primary qualities or Peircean convergence on explanatory hypotheses. But that is not what is worrying Wiggins here. He thinks that if you simply took desires ('concerns') as given, then 'cosmic' rationality would consist in an *a priori* schema or decision procedure for maximizing or optimizing their satisfaction. (That there could be such a schema is what the Prisoner's Dilemma paradox apparently refutes.) Wiggins thinks that when ends are not simply taken as given, but themselves are considered, or reasoned about, or deliberated on, with respect to their value, the possibility of one objective practical rationality disappears. But if this is not question-begging, then surely nothing in the world is. Why could there not be, in principle, a rational consensus about the value of ends? I do not mean any actually existing cross-cultural agreement of course nor, equally of course, do I mean that there will be agreement in value *commitments*. But then the view that value is essentially a function of commitment is one of those that Wiggins, too, is most interested in *opposing*. Surely there can be a rational consensus that, e.g., prudence, courage, honesty, and loyalty are virtues; that pleasure and happiness are goods; that pain and injury are evils, etc. And in doubtful or unclear cases (chastity, purity, nobility, great riches, unlimited power) arguments can be presented for or against their being virtues or goods, arguments that are capable of rational assessment. True, we cannot take ends simply as given. Ends can be appraised with respect to their value. However, no reason has been given, at least in the present context, why this could not be a matter of universal practical reason, valid for all.

(3) As has already been said, practical judgments (that I ought, that I should, that I'd better, etc.) are not and do not mark resolves or decisions. One must not confuse 'I ought to *x*' with 'I shall *x*'. What does it mean to say that I ought, all things considered, to *x*? It means that *x*-ing is the course of action best supported by reasons. And what does that mean? It means that there is more or greater or weightier value (more significant worth) to be gained (good to be obtained or increased or preserved, or evil to be avoided or lessened or overcome) by doing *x* than by doing anything else. This is not a matter of the world conforming to discourse. It is a matter of discourse conforming to the world. To say that there is more or

greater or weightier value to be gained by doing x than by not doing it or by doing anything else is to make a truth claim, and one that is open to rational assessment. Thus cognitivism is true. But naturalism is not, for naturalism leaves out what is distinctive or characteristic of value (desirability, goodness, worth), which is what gives it inherent practical relevance when the valuable object in question is one achievable by action. On this particular point, the non-cognitivists are right (cf. pp. 93–6 above).

(4) In some situations, rare as they may be, it really is impossible to say that this, clearly, among possible alternatives, is the course of action (or inaction) one ought to take. And that is because the reasons (values to be gained) are equally balanced on all sides. But because it is impossible to choose, on rational grounds, among two or more such equally well-supported (or ill-supported) alternatives, we are not compelled to say about each of them that it is (a) false that we ought, all things considered, to do it, and also (b) false that it is not the case that, all things considered, we ought to do it. The case is that we ought, all things considered, to choose one of them indifferently. So there is no violation of the law of excluded middle nor of that condition of regular truth.

One other possibility remains to be considered. Look once more at Wiggins' list of valuations (value-predicates): 'good', 'bad', 'beautiful', 'ugly', 'ignoble', 'brave', 'just', 'mischievous', 'malicious', 'worthy', 'honest', 'corrupt', 'disgusting', 'amusing', 'diverting', 'boring', 'dishonest', 'priggish' (1976: 388, 359). Now all of these words can be used in contexts of appraisal where deliberation or practical reasoning (concerning what one should do) is not what is at issue. I may simply be interested in appraising a work of art, or a person's (perhaps even a fictitious person's) character, or a historical political regime, or my own conduct in the past, where no question of *acting* on the basis of the appraisal can even arise. Yet according to Wiggins, practical judgments (that I ought, that I should, that I'd better, etc.) are 'directives' or decisions, by implication equivalent to 'Let me do x' or 'I shall do x'. Though valuations *can* be made in practical contexts ('can impinge upon practical appreciation and judgment'), practical judgments *by definition* are made in practical contexts.

What this overlooks or ignores is that 'ought' and 'should' judgments can also be made in contexts other than that of deliberation, indeed in contexts where no question of deciding what to do exists or can even arise. Thus 'I ought to have taken out insurance a year ago'; 'Napoleon should not have marched on Moscow'; 'Oliver ought not to have asked for more'. One can not only have more reason, here and now, for x-ing rather than not x-ing or doing anything else, one can also have *had* more reason at some time in the past for x-ing, etc., something about which now *nothing is to be done*. Furthermore I can, if asked to assume a casuistical role, tell you what I think you ought to do, or offer an opinion about a third person concerning what he or she ought to do. And the words 'ought', 'should', etc. are perfectly univocal across all these contexts. 'I ought to x' said by you, now, has the same truth (or other assertibility) conditions as 'You ought to x' said by me to you now. 'I ought to have done x last week when I first thought of it' said by me now has the same truth (or other assertibility) conditions as 'I ought to do this' said by me last week when I first thought of it. What further proof could there be that 'ought', 'should', etc. judgments do not express decisions or consist of 'directives'? Valuations and judgments that one ought, should, etc. are not *the very same*, but they do not have the difference Wiggins imagines them to have either.

Let us return to consider once more Wiggins' overall position *vis à vis* the element of (reconstituted) non-cognitivism remaining in valuations and in practical judgments. We must remember it is there in both (according to Wiggins), though valuational predicates stand for properties 'in a world'. His overall view, in so far as it can be distinguished, seems to be something like the following. Valuations are objective, and the assertibility condition of value predicates can even be said to amount to truth, provided 'truth' is interpreted broadly enough to include input from our 'concerns' (= desires), which should be no more distressing than supposing that the assertibility condition for the application of predicates like 'table' and 'yellow' and 'famine', amount to truth, since they involve how the world is for *us*. That the assertibility condition for practical judgments amounts to truth, however, is at least very dubious for the reasons given. Nevertheless even here, if we are to consider an analogy with Wittgenstein's conception of mathematics combined with constructivist or intuitionist views (Wiggins 1976: 371), we may be able to conclude that in practical judgments, as in mathematical statements, we have the compossibility of objectivity, discovery, *and* invention. Whether or not we decide to use the word 'true' here does not matter; nor need we fuss about 'regular' truth. So long as assertibility involves all three, that is all we really need. The possibility of life having meaning, which depends upon the element of discovery (cognition), is saved. We can accept much of what the non-cognitivist says, but we need no longer pay attention when he insists that value is a matter of invention and not of discovery, which, if it were true, would mean that our actions, hence our lives, had *no* meaning.

I would like to go further and expunge the element of non-cognitivism altogether, whether it is of the relativisitic or of the subjectivist sort. (That values are anthropocentric, or at least that they exist only for subject–agents, and that value qualities or properties are not *primary* qualities, I happily concede.) So far as valuations are concerned, the non-cognitivist threat is expressed in a passage already quoted: 'Perhaps all strict valuations of the more specific and interesting kind have the interesting property that the interpretation of the value predicate itself presupposes a shared viewpoint, and a set of concerns common between interpreter and subject' (1976: 364). This, Wiggins apparently thinks, puts the non-cognitivist position in a way that eliminates the need for a fact–value distinction, since (he thinks) he is not required to grant to this (reconstructed) non-cognitivist (supporter of the doctrine of cognitive underdetermination) that human values are invented and not discovered. (As he later reveals, he wants a bit of both.)

The key word here is 'concerns', a word that keeps cropping up again and again and which is also found in the writings of Bernard Williams (1975). What it means, of course, is *desires*, including interests (in the sense of what interests one, or what one is interested in), and probably valuations and known likes or dislikes (construed as objects of desire or avoidance) as well. In other words, it stands for *motivational propensities*. Now to treat desires or motivational propensities as one of the essential ingredients of *value,* or of grounding reasons and 'ought' claims, which are internally tied to value, is a fundamental error, as I argued at length in chapters 1–3. Certainly people's 'concerns' vary from culture to culture and, indeed, from individual to individual, but this does not take the thesis of cultural relativism forward by a single iota. Value is not *to any extent whatever* a function or product of desire. I have already criticized Wiggins for this in connection with his claim (as it might be paraphrased) that in order for value to be perceived or cognized, it must be true both that the objects conform to desire and desire to the objects. (There must be a 'fit'.) One of the things that permits non-cognitivism to erode the objectivist view that Wiggins clearly wishes to espouse, is his failure to see that, where value is concerned, motivational propensities are not even in the picture, except for the truth that to recognize something as being or possessing a value achievable by action is a sufficient condition of having at least a reflective desire to pursue it. Though our 'concerns' may be partly a consequence of our recognition of value, what has value for us and our recognition of it is not to any extent determined by our 'concerns'. Our concerns will, to some extent, conform to our apprehension of value. But the reverse is impossible.

As Williams sees it, appraisal can only have point if it relates to our 'concerns', and valuations are without point if they do not relate to 'real options', that is actual possibilities of choice (Williams 1975). Again, the central question is seen as 'What shall I do?', and practical philosophy (the only axiology there is) is seen as essentially providing answers to this question. Where it cannot, no real appraisal is going on. Compare Wiggins speaking for the (reconstructed) non-cognitivist on the impossibility of practical judgments being true or false:

When we judge that this is what we must do now, or that that is what we'd better do, or that our life must now take one direction rather than another direction, we are not fitting truths (or even probabilities) into a pattern where any discrepancy proves that we have mistaken falsehood for a truth. Often we have to make a practical choice which another rational agent might understand through and through, not fault or even disagree with, but (as Winch has stressed) make differently himself; whereas, if there is disagreement over what is factually true and two rational men have come to different conclusions, then we think it has to be theoretically possible to uncover some discrepancy in their respective view of the evidence. . . . But in matters of practice we are grateful for the existence of alternative answers. The choice between them is then up to us. Here is our freedom. . . . In living a life there is no truth, and there is nothing *like* regular truth for us to aim at (1976: 367).[2]

Wiggins finds this very worrying and believes he must somehow accomodate it. Note what it says (1) Deciding what we'd better do

[2]There are footnote references, first to Williams (1966), where Williams refers to Hartmann's claim that good, lying in a large number of incompatible directions, is impossible to achieve wholly and without compromise, and then to Winch (1965).

or what we must do (he prefers 'must' to 'ought' because, as he supposes, 'must' and 'must not', unlike 'ought' and 'ought not' are genuine contraries, not because he is thinking exclusively in terms of moral obligation), is not a matter of fitting a truth into a consistent pattern of truths. (Essentially the same point is expressed in the final sentence.) (2) Two rational men may in identical circumstances, make different decisions concerning what turn their life should take, yet each may understand and have complete sympathy with the other – all consistent with their rationality. It is, in some important sense, 'up to them' what they shall choose. The first of these points is just one more example of the confusion between deciding what we should, ought, must, or had better do (the course of action best supported by reasons or supported by the best reasons), i.e. deliberation, and deciding (making up our minds) what we *shall* do. And, of course, we need not decide to do what, in our own judgment, is the course of action best supported by reasons; we may decide to act (or remain passive) in order to satisfy some contrary and more powerful inclination. (This confusion has already been dealt with.)

As to the second point, certainly one 'rational person' (sound practical reasoner who acts in accord with his judgments), consistent with his rationality, can say of another that he understands why that person is making the choice he is making and that his reasons are perfectly sound, but had he been in those circumstances, for different reasons, the choice would have been otherwise. There is nothing problematic here *if* we assume that the two persons have different preferences (in the strictly correct sense of *likings*, as opposed to desirings) or find value in different things or find greater or lesser value in the same things. This will almost certainly be the case, since no two persons agree entirely in what they find to their liking, or what they prefer, or what they find more or less interesting or absorbing, or what they otherwise find value in and how much they find there. Of course what this means is that each does what she ought to do, given what is valuable (or thought with reason to be valuable) for herself. That is why each can be fully rational yet entirely sympathetic and supportive of the other's decision. It is not the case that *the very same* reasons (tied to values to be gained) exist in both cases, while nevertheless leaving an option of choice (freedom). But if their situations were thoroughly identical, even including personal preferences, etc., then if one of them ought to take a certain course of action, the same is true of the other. There would be no room for 'freedom' then.

Notice again that Wiggins calls 'ought', 'should', 'must', 'had better', etc. judgments *practical* judgments or *directives*, and says that they mark *decisions* what to do. Another word that springs to mind here as being in this same category is '*prescriptions*', for what we are with here faced is a remnant of prescriptivism. But there is no need for it whatever. To say that one ought or should do something is to say that one has a reason, tied to a value (which can be specified) for doing it. To say that one ought, *all things considered*, or that one ought, *here and now* (or there and then) to do something, is to say that, on balance, this is the course of action best supported by reasons or supported by the best reasons (the most important values). And this is not a matter of decision, or choice, or commitment, or the having of 'pro-attitudes', but of a rational examination and comparison of goods to be gained and evils to be avoided or overcome. Furthermore it seems to me that this is essentially the way Wiggins would *rather* have it; his intuitions are in order, but he is dogged by this unfortunate remnant of non-cognitivist prescriptivism.

Williams too, by his treatment of 'concerns' (i.e. desires) as central in evaluation and practical reasoning, and his insistence upon relating all practical questions to the question 'What shall I do?', hence to decision-making, 'options', etc., also betrays his non-cognitivist ancestry. He, however, at least has the excuse that he does not, like Wiggins, wish to argue for the objectivity of value, nor does he regard this objectivity as a necessary (let alone sufficient) condition of life's having a meaning or significance. Desire-satisfaction is perfectly adequate for him.

Furthermore we can see the whole distressing syndrome – how to be a non-cognitivist without actually being a non-cognitivist – with its fishing about in the philosophy of mathematics for an appropriate parallel, as stemming from the continued belief that desire must somehow be, if not the source, then at least a necessary condition of value. Thus talk of the 'fit' between desire and its objects (the good), and the tying of 'ought', etc. judgments to decision and action, hence to motivation, hence to desire ('concerns'). Wiggins would be home free, and he could have his objective values, if he would only sever the supposedly necessary tie with desire, in the case of value predicates, and with decision, hence action (an inheritance from prescriptivism) in the case of so-called practical judgments. Of course if one judges that one ought to do something (that one has a reason for doing it), one has, as a necessary consequence, a reflective desire to do it. But that, as has long since been noted, is another thing altogether.

But let us return to the question whether there are any objects attainable by action of sufficient value to make our actions worth our while and our lives worth living. The existence of objective value, not just in my sense of being objectively determinable and independent of desire and will, but as somehow lying in objects to be discovered there and sought (or contemplated), is, according to Wiggins, the necessary and sufficient condition of our actions', our experiences', and hence our lives' having meaning or significance. (That is why non-cognitivism, some form of which he thinks he is obliged to accept, worries him so much, and why he attempts to defuse it). Hedonic value will not do for him, since it is located in subjective states, yet 'disgusting', 'amusing', 'diverting', 'boring', appear on his list of (presumably) characteristic value predicates; indeed they constitute a full quarter of the values mentioned on his initial list. There is a clear inconsistency here, for it could not be claimed that it was an objective quality or property of a thing (or even that it is perceived as such by the person who is disgusted, diverted, bored, etc.), to be amusing and so forth. It could at best be a dispositional property (to amuse, disgust, etc.) or one might attempt to give such attributes objectivity by saying that a thing is not *really* amusing (disgusting, etc.) unless one *ought* to be amused (disgusted, etc.) by it. Here, by implication, there is some perceivable attribute to which a certain reaction is appropriate, but being disgusting (etc.) is not that attribute itself. Yet being amusing, diverting, disgusting, etc., *are* values, values of the hedonic kind. They are, furthermore, values that are quite genuine and objective in my primary sense, being independent of will and desire. That an object, or experience, or activity, has such a character for us must be discovered. That the character itself has positive or negative value is something we know in knowing what it *is*. And though that is not discovery, it is not invention either!

And unlike feeling good and feeling bad, they involve, except in the case of sensations, an intentional relationship with the real world. (Otherwise, as 'false pleasures', their value is significantly less.) Surely the having or gaining of positive values of this kind *is* sufficient to make life worth living, one might suppose. Indeed a life consisting of nothing but the innocent pursuit of pleasure is our very picture of paradise! But we do not live in paradise (no matter how desirable that might be), and the pure life of pleasure (and the avoidance of its opposite) here on earth is still a life without meaning or significance, especially since, unlike paradise, where everyone is immortal, every individual life is short and its possibilities – even of pleasure – limited. Life's exigencies make virtue necessary (there is no need for virtue in paradise and no possibility of vice) and the very conditions of individual human existence constitute a challenge, not just to lead a life as full of joys and as free of sorrows as possible, but to achieve some measure of excellence in the short time one is here. In addition to moral virtue, which is for the good of others and of society, as well as of oneself, there are various talents, abilities, and skills (including taste and aesthetic perception, which brings special rewards) that can be developed. Often, as in the case of the various trades and occupations, they have a socially useful end – the more developed the more useful, and always, of course, directed toward their proper end – but the end may be aesthetic, as in the case of artistic skills, talents, and abilities, whether of the creative, recreative, or appreciative kind, or in some cases, e.g. gymnastics, chess, a skill or talent can be developed simply for its own sake.

Let us look at the other value-predicates on Wiggins' list. 'Good' and 'bad' are quite general. Furthermore there is no property of 'goodness' or 'badness' as such, as Elizabeth Anscombe has quite rightly said. Things possess certain qualities which are good or bad, or things are good or bad in a certain respect. 'Beautiful' and 'ugly' are aesthetic values and, as such, have some claim to objectivity of the kind that Wiggins feels must be attributed to all value properties. The remainder, namely 'ignoble', 'brave', 'just', 'mischievous', 'malicious', 'worthy', 'honest', 'corrupt', 'dishonest', 'priggish', are moral predicates, connected to one or other of the virtues or vices or to virtue and vice in general. And as such they are things to aim at or achieve or preserve, or avoid or get rid of, as the case may be – all as part of the pursuit of virtue or excellence.

Not only is every individual life impermanent, with the

consequence that nothing is to be gained by anyone once and for all, but, as Taylor rightly points out, all monuments perish, and nothing can be brought into being to remain forever. Taylor thinks that this would make life meaningless except for the magic elixir of desire, but as Wiggins quite rightly notes, one cannot *reflectively* desire or continue to desire a thing if one does not see it as worthwhile. And desire itself cannot be so seen, Taylor to the contrary notwithstanding. Thus there are no accomplishments that endure forever, no individual life that does not end in death, and also no value or worth to be derived from desire. Is suicide, then, the only rational act? Certainly not. But we must not aim at that which we know is impossible of accomplishment, for that is a paradigm of irrationality. Thus we should not aim at either permanence or immortality; nor should we build (literally or metaphorically) on the assumption that we will be able to keep forever what we acquire. And there are other things which we may believe to be good but which are not, and to which we should not, therefore, devote our lives. Wealth, for example, is certainly good *as a means,* but the accumulation of wealth *for its own sake,* without using it for anything, on the assumption that it is inherently valuable (perhaps the only thing that is!), or that one can keep it forever, is a paradigm of an irrational end. The same is true of power, which is also good as a means, but irrational (not to say evil) to seek or exercise for its own sake. Similarly devotion to sensual pleasure as the sole end of action will lead at best to disappointment and at worst to evil and corruption, since sensual appetites, if singly pursued, become more and more difficult to satisfy. (This is a matter of empirical psychology.) Prestige or status too is inherently desirable, but only to the extent that it is merited; otherwise it is living a lie, a lie which includes self-deception, and is not to be aimed at by a rational person *for its own sake,* no matter how useful it may be as a means. The achievement of excellence will, other things being equal, confer status or prestige as an added benefit. But it is excellence that one is to pursue, not the status that has inherent value only as its reward. And all of this, I make haste to say, is very ancient wisdom.

References

Anscombe, G. E. M. 1957. *Intention*, Oxford and Ithaca, N.Y.

Anscombe, G. E. M. 1958. Modern moral philosophy, *Philosophy* **33**, 1–19

Aristotle. *Nicomachean Ethics*

Beehler, Rodger 1978. *Moral Life*, Oxford

Bond, E. J. 1966. Moral requirement and the need for deontic language, *Philosophy* **41**, 233–49

Bond, E. J. 1968. The supreme principle of morality, *Dialogue* **7**, 167–79

Bond, E. J. 1974. Reasons, wants, and values, *Canadian Journal of Philosophy* **3**, 333–47

Bond, E. J. 1979. Desire, action, and the good, *American Philosophical Quarterly* **16**, 53–9

Bond, E. J. 1981. On desiring the desirable, *Philosophy* **56**, 489–96

Bond, E. J. and Gewirth, Alan 1980. Symposium on reason and morality, *Metaphilosophy* **11**, 36–75

Chisholm, R. M. 1966. Freedom and action. In *Freedom and Determinism*, ed. Keith Lehrer. New York

Davidson, Donald 1963. Actions, reasons, and causes, *Journal of Philosophy* **60**, 685–700

Foot, Philippa 1958. Moral beliefs, *Proceedings of the Aristotelian Society* **59**, 83–104. (Reprinted in Foot 1979. Page references are to this.)

Foot, Philippa 1972a. Morality as a system of hypothetical imperatives, *Philosophical Review* **81**. (Reprinted in Foot 1979. Page references are to this.)

Foot, Philippa 1972b. Reasons for action and desires, *Proceedings of the Aristotelian Society, Supplementary Volume* **46**. (Reprinted, with an additional note, in Foot 1979. Page references are to this.)

Foot, Philippa 1979. *Virtues and Vices*, Oxford

Gert, Bernard 1970. *The Moral Rules*, New York. (The text was slightly revised and new prefaces were added in the 1st [1973] and the 2nd [n.d.] Torchbook editions. Quotations are from the last of these. The pagination is the same in all editions.)

Gewirth, Alan 1978. *Reason and Morality*, Chicago

Grice, Geoffrey Russell 1967. *The Grounds of Moral Judgement*, Cambridge

Hare, R. M. 1952. *The Language of Morals*, Oxford

Hare, R. M. 1972. Wrongness and harm. In *Essays on the Moral Concepts*, pp. 92–109. London

Harman, Gilbert 1975. Moral relativism defended, *Philosophical Review* **84**, 3–22

Harman, Gilbert 1977. *The Nature of Morality*, New York
Harman, Gilbert 1978. Relativistic ethics: morality as politics. In *Midwest Studies in Philosophy III*, ed. P. French *et al.* Morris, Minnesota
Hume, David 1739. *A Treatise of Human Nature*, London
Kant, Immanuel 1785. *Grundlegung zur Metaphysik der Sitten*, Riga
Locke, Don 1974. Reasons, wants, and causes, *American Philosophical Quarterly* 11, 169–79
Mackie, J. L. 1977. *Ethics: Inventing Right and Wrong*, Harmondsworth
McDowell, John 1978. Are moral requirements hypothetical imperatives? *Proceedings of the Aristotelian Society, Supplementary Volume* 52, 13–29
Mill, John Stuart 1861. Utilitarianism, *Fraser's Magazine* (3 parts). (Page references are to the edition by Oskar Piest, New York 1957.)
Nagel, Thomas 1970. *The Possibility of Altruism*, Oxford
Nagel, Thomas 1977. The fragmentation of value. In *Knowledge, Value and Belief*, ed. H. Tristram Engelhardt Jr and Daniel Callahan, Hastings-on-Hudson, N. Y. (Reprinted in Nagel 1979.)
Nagel, Thomas 1979. *Mortal Questions*, Cambridge
Nagel, Thomas 1980. The limits of objectivity. In *The Tanner Lectures on Human Values, Vol I*, ed. Sterling McMurrin, pp. 77–139. Salt Lake City and Cambridge
Narveson, Jan 1967. *Morality and Utility*, Baltimore
Nowell-Smith, P. H. 1954. *Ethics*, Harmondsworth
Phillips, D. Z. and Mounce, H. O. 1970. *Moral Practices*, London
Plato. *The Republic*
Rawls, John 1971. *A Theory of Justice*, Cambridge, Mass.
Richards, David A. J. 1971. *A Theory of Reasons for Action*, Oxford
Searle, John R. 1964. How to derive 'ought' from 'is', *Philosophical Review* 73, 43–58
Skinner, B. F. 1971. *Beyond Freedom and Dignity*, New York
Spinoza, Benedict de 1677. *Ethica*, Amsterdam
Spinoza, Benedict de. *De Intellectus Emendatione*
Taylor, Richard 1966. *Action and Purpose*, Englewood Cliffs, N. J.
Taylor, Richard 1970. *Good and Evil*, New York
Toulmin, S. E. 1950. *An Examination of the Place of Reason in Ethics*, Cambridge
Von Wright, G. H. 1963. *The Varieties of Goodness*, London
Wiggins, David 1976. Truth, invention, and the meaning of life, *Proceedings of the British Academy* 62, 331–78
Williams, Bernard 1966. Consistency and realism, *Proceedings of the Aristotelian Society, Supplementary Volume* 40, 1–22. (Reprinted in Williams 1973.)
Williams, Bernard 1972. *Morality: An Introduction to Ethics*, New York
Williams, Bernard 1973. *Problems of the Self*, Cambridge
Williams, Bernard 1975. The truth in relativism, *Proceedings of the Aristotelian Society* 75, 215–28
Williams, Bernard 1979. Internal and external reasons. In *Rational Action*, ed. Ross Harrison, pp. 17–28. Cambridge
Winch, Peter 1965. The universalizability of moral judgments, *The Monist* 49, 196–214

Index

Aesthetic value, 37, 64, 75, 88, 97, 140–2, 146, 160
Akrasia, 2, 25, 29, 79, 80
Altruism, 4
Anscombe, G.E.M., ix, 47–8, 52–5, 69, 160
Appetite/inclination/aversion, 11–21, 28–9, 41, 49–53, 56, 58–9, 66–7, 72–4, 85, 87, 94–5, 97, 104–6, 138, 140–1, 151, 157
Aristotle, 105, 140, 148–9
Aversion, *see* Appetite
Axiology, 1, 43, 84, 136, 138, 156
  See also Hedonism, axiological

Beehler, Rodger, 3–5, 33, 69–70, 75, 77–91
Belief, false, 46–50, 52, 54, 59
Bentham, Jeremy, 51, 103, 130, 137–8
Bond, E. J., 16, 77–8, 82n
Brahms, Johannes, 35–9, 43, 47, 63

Causes, reasons as, 21–6
Chisholm, R. M., 23
Choice, freedom of, 157–8
Choice, rational, 6
Cognition, 3–4, 6–7, 11–12, 14, 19–20, 33–4, 58–61, 67–8, 72–3, 82–3, 92, 138, 144–5
Cognitive underdetermination, 149–51, 155
Cognitivism, 153
Commitments, 152
Concerns, 70, 85, 101n, 155–8
Considerations, 4, 12–14, 106
Cultural relativism, 101, 155

Davidson, Donald, 21
Death, 21, 28, 89, 126–9, 136, 161
Deliberation, 1–5, 10, 14–15, 21, 31–5, 59–60, 62, 66, 68, 94, 151, 157
  See also Rationality, deliberative

Desire
  conscious, 16
  inclinational, *see* Inclination
  reflective, 15, 20–1, 41, 45, 55–9, 66, 71–3, 87, 94–5, 97, 104, 141, 156, 159, 161
  motivated/unmotivated, 11–14, 17
  rational, 6, 124
Desire-satisfaction, 2–9, 12, 15, 19, 24–5, 31, 43–50, 58, 61, 67, 72–3, 111–13, 118–19, 123–6, 133, 136–8, 144–7, 158
Disability, 128–9, 131–3

Emotions/emotional state, 17, 20, 22–3, 26, 29, 49, 53, 56
Empiricism, 96
Ends/means, 1, 3–4, 10–20, 24, 32, 43, 48, 54, 58, 60–1, 71–2, 86–7, 152
Ends, reflective, 15
Epicurus, 128
Ethics, 1, 7, 106, 136
Evil(s), 1, 40, 43, 46n, 70, 86, 88–9, 92, 94, 104, 123–30, 144, 152, 158, 160–1
  as deprivation of good(s), 131–5
  See also Pain
Excellence, 121–2, 134–5, 137, 148, 160–1
Excluded Middle, Law of, 151, 153
Existentialism, 147

Fact/value relationship, 93, 148, 150–1
Foot, Philippa, 4–5, 13–14, 27, 37, 42, 55, 69, 73–7, 90, 93
Freedom, 129–32

Gert, Bernard, 126–34
Gewirth, Alan, 82, 82n, 86n, 123–5, 129, 131, 133
Goodness, 5, 7, 19, 43, 47, 84, 110–11
Good(s), 1–2, 4, 6–7, 18, 42–3, 45–57,

88, 92, 104–5, 109, 111–12, 116,
120–1, 123–35, 140, 143–4, 149,
152, 158, 160
basic, 86n, 123, 131, 133, 135
common, 61n, 61–4, 74, 98–9, 130,
133
deprivation of, *see* Evil(s)
intrinsic, *see* Value(s), intrinsic
non-subtractive, 133
personal, 39, 43, 54–5, 60, 62–3, 73,
96–7, 101–2, 134–5
primary, 86n, 124, 133
Grice, Russell, viii, 37n
Guilt, 118

Hare, R. M., 137–8, 138n, 141
Harman, Gilbert, 3, 5, 20, 33, 55, 69, 75,
77, 91, 101, 101n, 145
Hartmann, N., 156n
Hedonic value, 46, 87, 93–5, 98–9, 102,
108, 110–11, 120, 123, 141, 146–7,
159
Hedonism, 45–6, ch. 6, 137–8, 143–4,
147
aesthetic, 64
axiological, 106–8, 110–11
ethical, 106
psychological, 105–8
tautological, 107, 109, 112
See also Pleasure
Hitler, Adolf, 70
Hume, David, 3, 12, 15, 58, 66–8, 73, 96

Idealism, 119
Immorality, 80–1
Inclination, *see* Appetite
Intentional object, 22–3, 26, 142
Intuition/intuitionism, 85–7, 89, 107–9,
119, 154
Irrationality, 28–30, 35, 62, 70, 73–4,
79–80, 126–8, 130, 161

James, Henry, 33, 38
Judgment, error, 52
Judgment, practical, 84, 136, 148–59
Justice, 76, 90–1

Kant, Immanuel, 10–11, 69n, 138

Leisure/work, 113–17, 120–1
Life, intrinsic value, 89, 117–18, 128–9,
131, 136–7, 139, 142–4, 146–9, 155,
158–61

Locke, Don, 71
Love, 2

Mackie, J. L., 3, 20, 54–5, 61, 84–5, 138
MacNiven, C. D., 98n
Mathematics, 150, 154, 158
McDowell, John, 55, 56n, 71
Meinongianism, 89
Mill, J. S., 98, 98n, 103–9, 137, 141
Mind/mental state, 26, 99
Moore, G. E., 99–100
Moral requirements, 39, 53, 64, 66, 68–
70, 74–7, 79, 101, 110, 112–13, 115,
118, 157
Moral values, 2, 33, 68, 78, 80, 84, 92, 95
deontic, 64, 69–70, 74–9, 81–3, 90–1,
94, 96, 102, 119
Morality, 1, 6, 8, 19, 65, 69, 104, 135
objective, 2, 5–6, 12
universal, 33
Motivation
moral, 10–11
rational, 1, 2, 9, 15, 18, 21, 29–30, 36,
40, 56–61, 95, 106, 108, 115, 117
See also Reasons, motivating
reflective, 18, 53
unconscious, 16
Motivational propensities, 3–5, 11–14,
32, 34, 39–42, 62, 78, 93, 101, 140,
155–6
Mounce, H. O., 101

Nagel, Thomas, 4–5, 7, 11–14, 17–18,
27, 36–7, 42–3, 49, 58, 60, 61n, 64,
64n, 67–8, 68n, 71, 73, 82–3, 83n,
91
Narveson, Jan, 105–13, 115, 118–19
Nathanson, Stephen, ix, 52n
Naturalism, 93, 95–6, 153
Needs, 46n, 131, 133, 135
Nietzsche, Friedrich, 119
Non-cognitivism, 41, 93, 95–6, 108,
111, 137–9, 143, 146–50, 153–6,
158–9
Nowell-Smith, Patrick, 108

'Owen Wingrave', 33–5, 37–9, 62–3

Pain/suffering/misery, 28, 102–3, 123–
34, 136, 152
avoidance, 111, 125
Parfit, Derek, 61n, 64n
Peircean convergence, 148, 152

Phenomenalism, 96
Phillips, D. Z., 101
Plato, 135, 138
Platonism, 58, 85, 87, 89, 92, 109–10, 119, 134
Pleasure, 35–9, 44–7, 49–51, 59–62, 64, 67, 87–8, 94, 98–9, 102–7, 113–22, 126–9, 136–7, 141, 147, 152, 159–60
   loss of, 130–4
Power, 161
Prescriptivism, 158–9
Prisoner's Dilemma Paradox, 152
'Pro-attitudes', 85, 93, 100, 108, 111, 158
Propositional attitudes, 16, 22, 27
Prudence, 4, 19, 25, 36, 43, 65–6, 68, 73–4, 78–9, 83, 89, 96, 102, 152
Purpose-fulfilment, 123–5, 131, 133

Rationality
   deliberative, 15, 18, 21, 40–1, 54, 57–8
   objective, 6–7, 12
   practical, 1, 6, 8, 24, 31, 40, 88, 95, 151–2, 157
Rawls, John, 5, 43, 45, 64, 70, 73, 86n, 98, 119, 124, 126, 129, 133, 145
Reasons
   external, 13–15, 32–8, 65–71, 75–6
   grounding, 27–32, 37, 40–2, 46, 48, 53, 56–60, 65–6, 75–6, 91, 106–8, 112, 115, 117, 127, 134–5, 155
   internal, 33, 42, 48, 60, 65–9, 71, 91, 149
   motivating, 28, 31, 37, 42, 53, 58
   universal, 8, 38
Reflection, rational, 14, 64–8, 71–2, 144
Respect/self-respect, 121, 133, 148
Richards, David, A. J., 5–6, 32, 64, 69–70, 73–4, 76, 90, 124, 145
Russell, Bertrand, 96

Sartre, Jean-Paul, 93, 137–8
Searle, John R., 93
Self-consciousness, 106n
Self-interest, 19, 64, 66, 68–9, 72, 80, 88–90, 102
Selfishness, 118
Sensation, 142, 147, 159
Skinner, B. F., 24
Spinoza, Benedict de, 99, 103
Subjects/subjective states, 22–6, 32, 61n, 96, 99–100, 102–3, 123, 138–41, 144–5, 152, 155

Taylor, Charles, 51n
Taylor, Richard, 3, 23, 137–8, 140–1, 143, 145, 147, 161
Toulmin, Stephen, 101
Truth, 27, 106, 153–7

Utilitarianism, 83n, 111–13, 117–19, 137, 145
   hedonistic, 138, 144–5
Utility, 20, 42, 54–5, 86–8, 111

Value assertions, 142–3, 146
Value judgments, 53, 84, 95–6, 138–9, 141, 147, 149
Value predicates, 158–60
Value(s)
   common, see Good(s), common
   instrumental, 32, 58, 72, 86
   intrinsic, 107–12, 114, 116, 118–21
   ontological/epistemological status, 55, 84–101
   personal, see Good(s), personal
   phenomenal objectivity, 139–42, 146, 149
   undiscovered, 35–9, 43–4, 47, 61, 97
   universal, 8, 38, 55
   universally shared, see Good(s), common
Vice, 160
Virtue, 55, 106, 121–2, 134–5, 148, 152, 160
Von Wright, 123–5, 131, 135

Want-satisfaction, see Desire-satisfaction
Wealth, 161
Well-being, 4, 12, 14, 66–8, 73–4, 82–3, 88–9
Wickedness, 80
Wiggins, David, 55, 136, 138–50, 152–6, 158–61
Will, 3–4, 11–12, 25–6, 58, 71, 80, 84, 95, 99, 137–8, 142, 146, 151, 159
   freedom of, 9, 24
Williams, Bernard, ix, 3, 14, 19, 27, 32–7, 42, 46–8, 50, 55, 58, 62–3, 67–9, 71, 73, 75, 77, 91, 101, 101n, 155–6, 156n, 158
Winch, Peter, 156, 156n
Wittgenstein, Ludwig, 101, 150, 154
Work, see Leisure